Palmetto Rose

Social Fictions Series

Scope

The *Social Fictions* series emerges out of the arts-based research movement. The series includes full-length fiction books that are informed by social research but written in a literary/artistic form (novels, plays, and short story collections). Believing there is much to learn through fiction, the series only includes works written entirely in the literary medium adapted. Each book includes an academic introduction that explains the research and teaching that informs the book as well as how the book can be used in college courses. The books are underscored with social science or other scholarly perspectives and intended to be relevant to the lives of college students—to tap into important issues in the unique ways that artistic or literary forms can.

Please consult www.patricialeavy.com for submission requirements (click the book series tab).

VOLUME 29

The titles published in this series are listed at *brill.com/soci*

Palmetto Rose

By

J. E. Sumerau

BRILL

SENSE

LEIDEN | BOSTON

All chapters in this book have undergone peer review.

The Library of Congress Cataloging-in-Publication Data is available online at
http://catalog.loc.gov

ISSN 2542-8799
ISBN 978-90-04-39051-5 (paperback)
ISBN 978-90-04-39220-5 (hardback)
ISBN 978-90-04-39221-2 (e-book)

ADVANCE PRAISE FOR
PALMETTO ROSE

Honestly written and full of hope for anyone who has loved and lost. You can't help but fall in love with *Palmetto Rose*'s narrator as you learn about their efforts to come back from losing their first love. The reader will gain a glimpse into the narrator's early adulthood – their struggles with intimacy, their resilience, and the rich family of choice that helps them through it all. The relationships articulated in these pages offer a model for navigating poly love, friendship and disappointment with a commitment to patience and care. An engaging read for all who dare envision the expansive possibilities of family.
Katie Acosta, Ph.D., Georgia State University and author of *Amigas y Amantes: Sexually Nonconforming Latinas Negotiate Family*

In *Palmetto Rose*, Sumerau continues the compellingly complex story of the narrator we meet in their first novel, *Cigarettes & Wine*. *Palmetto Rose* explores the lives, loves, and losses of a diverse range of queer young adults living in the south, generating a narrative rich in detail and description that provides a much-needed portrayal of the ways that individuals in polyamorous relationships navigate relationships with one another and with their metamours.
Brandy Simula, Ph.D., Emory University

This was a perfect read for me – much like the "Perfect Palmetto Rose." Sumerau's novel reintroduces us to "Kid" whose fluid gender identity and bisexuality interact with characters who are deeply immersed in friendships that are also fluid-and ever-changing. Readers can't help but notice the ease in which Sumerau weaves discussions of polyamory, asexuality, queer and transgender identities into Kid's everyday interactions. The reader is (happily) forced to dismiss taken-for-granted assumptions about gender and sexuality because Kid does – Kid guides the reader through the life of their friends – sometimes of discrimination and tragic loss, but more often lives about love and new friendships. Kid is at times disparaging about their educational abilities all the while they teach us, the reader, more about gender and sexuality fluid relationships than any other character I have met.

Andrea Miller, Ph.D., Webster University

In *Palmetto Rose,* Sumerau shares the story of young adults navigating romantic relationships and life on their own in Atlanta, Georgia. We follow the characters as they discover how their previous individual and collective experiences impact their current relationships and worldviews. Sumerau beautifully captures the complications of early adulthood for characters defying gender and sexual binaries in the early 2000s. This novel, similar to Sumerau's other works, highlights the stories of bisexual, genderfluid, transgender, and poly people that are often missing from mainstream fiction. *Palmetto Rose* also serves as a great supplemental text for courses addressing gender identities, sexualities, religion, families, culture, and the South.

Mandi N. Barringer, Ph.D., University of North Florida

Prepare to be unreachable for at least a day because once you start *Palmetto Rose*, you won't be able to put it down. In a much-anticipated sequel to *Cigarettes & Wine*, Sumerau thrusts us back into the world of Lena, Abs, Kid, and their family of choice in Atlanta in the years after the loss of a beloved member of the family. We follow Kid as they reconnect to their past and begin the process of healing and finding new love within and beyond themselves. Bursting with poetic prose and multifaceted new characters, *Palmetto Rose* marks what will be some of the best queer fiction and sociology of the year. *Palmetto Rose* continues Sumerau's legacy of writing heart wrenching *and* warming tales of young adulthood that double as an indispensable tool for teaching in the social sciences, art, and humanities.

Lain A. B. Mathers, Doctoral Candidate, University of Illinois Chicago

Previous Novels by J. E. Sumerau

Cigarettes & Wine

Essence

Homecoming Queens

That Year

Other People's Oysters
(with Alexandra C. H. Nowakowski)

To Nik for reminding me to look forward to each new chapter in the course of a life and convincing me there had to be more to this story

CONTENTS

Preface   xiii

Acknowledgements   xvii

Chapter 1   1

Chapter 2   7

Chapter 3   15

Chapter 4   21

Chapter 5   27

Chapter 6   35

Chapter 7   41

Chapter 8   49

Chapter 9   55

Chapter 10   61

Chapter 11   67

Chapter 12   73

Chapter 13   79

Chapter 14   87

Chapter 15   93

Chapter 16   99

Chapter 17   107

Chapter 18   113

CONTENTS

Chapter 19   119

Chapter 20   125

Chapter 21   131

Chapter 22   137

Chapter 23   145

Chapter 24   151

Chapter 25   157

Suggested Classroom or Book Club Use   161

About the Author   163

PREFACE

Imagine engaging in sexual intimacy with someone you care about for the first time after surviving the loss of a serious, committed, loving relationship.

In *Palmetto Rose*, this is where we find a bi+, gender fluid narrator affectionately called Kid by their loved ones. After five years trying to numb and escape the pain of losing their first love to a tragic accident, Kid begins to wake up, grieve, and try to rebuild their life in Atlanta, Georgia. Through their eyes, we watch as they seek to make sense of grief, pursue the possibility of a college education, and embark on their first serious romantic relationship since they were a teenager. In the process, we spend time with their chosen family of friends who navigate relationships, graduate programs, and developing careers. As the story unfolds, these friends face the ups and downs of early adulthood alongside the ways their individual and shared pasts find voices in their current endeavors, future plans, and intertwined lives. Although many characters in this story originally appeared in *Cigarettes & Wine*, *Homecoming Queens*, or *Other People's Oysters*, *Palmetto Rose* may be read as a stand-alone novel.

Although written as a first-person narrative that allows readers to imagine themselves in the shoes of the narrator, *Palmetto Rose* is a novel about the life course and early adulthood; how we shift and change in relation to the events we experience in the past and hope for in the future, and how the people, places, narratives, and emotional experiences we face shape our impressions of our lives, the social world, and the passage of time. It is also a case study of the complexity of gender, sexuality, age, religion, emotion, region, and broader social norms in the formation and change of identities, relationships, and selves over the life course. As in life, the ways our varied intersections, relationships and experiences impact the life course permeate the events captured in the following pages. *Palmetto Rose* offers a view into the ways young people with both deeply positive loving bonds and shared painful losses grow into adults throughout their twenties, and the ways such people may shift over time in response to individual and collective experiences, intersections, and relationships that arise in the course of their lives. It also provides a first-person view of the ways emotions, intimacy, college access and experience, healthcare norms, families, friends, lovers, and broader social norms influence the life course and early adulthood.

Palmetto Rose also follows my prior *Social Fictions* work by highlighting realistic portrayals of bisexual, transgender, and poly experiences all too rarely available in contemporary media or academic materials. Alongside academic and media portrayals of the world that generally only notice binary options, it delivers a reminder that non-binary sexual, gender and relationship options exist, and introduces readers to some of the conflicts unique to such groups (and shared by other nonconformists) in early adulthood. Especially at a time when even college professors sometimes struggle with topics related to fluidity and when LGBTQIA students at book talks regularly ask me for more options for reading and learning about our lives, *Palmetto Rose* supplies readers with an opportunity to view the world, society, college and early adulthood through the eyes of a fluid narrator.

While entirely fictional, *Palmetto Rose* is grounded in my own personal experience as a bisexual (on the pansexual end of the spectrum), non-binary transwoman (formerly identified as a cross-dresser, transsexual, genderqueer, and/or transwoman at different points), and poly (with a preference for an open relationship with one or more primary, committed partnerships) person raised in the south. It is also built upon years of ethnographic, auto-ethnographic, historical and statistical research I have done concerning intersections of sexualities, gender, religion, and health in the United States, and hundreds of formal and informal interviews I have conducted – professionally and for personal interest – with bisexual (across the spectrum), transgender (throughout the umbrella), lesbian, gay, asexual, heterosexual, intersex, poly (in varied forms), kink, cisgender and Queer identified people who span the religious-nonreligious spectrum and were raised all over the world. Since stories are often powerful pedagogical tools for stimulating reflection and discussion about even the most challenging topics, I crafted this novel as a way for readers to step into the shoes of a fluid person, and in so doing, acquire a starting point for understanding sexual, gender, and relationship complexity in society.

For me, *Palmetto Rose* is a pedagogical text blending artistic and research efforts in a manner that has, throughout my career thus far, been incredibly effective in classrooms. In fact, the reactions to my earlier *Social Fictions* endeavors from students and fellow teachers led me to craft this story as an expansion of the lives of the characters introduced in prior novels. As such, *Palmetto Rose* may be used as an educational tool for people seeking to better understand growing numbers of openly bisexual, transgender, and poly people; as a supplemental reading for courses across disciplines dealing with gender, sexualities, relationships, families, the life course, narratives, emotions, the American south, identities, culture, and/or intersectionality; or it can, of course, be read entirely for pleasure.

ACKNOWLEDGEMENTS

Thank you to Patricia Leavy, Peter de Liefde, John Bennett, Jolanda Karada, Paul Chambers, and everyone else at Brill | Sense and the *Social Fictions* series for your faith in me, your willingness to support creativity, and your invaluable guidance. I would also like to especially thank Shalen Lowell for your considerable assistance and support. I cannot overstate how much the efforts and support of all you means to me.

Thank you especially to my spouse Xan Nowakowski for giving me the courage to write novels in the first place and walking by my side as I completed them and sent them out for consideration. My books would not exist without your inspiration, guidance, and faith, and I will never be able to thank you enough for what your support and encouragement means to me.

I would also like to thank Lain Mathers, Nik Lampe, Eve Haydt, and Shay Phillips for providing constructive comments and insights throughout this process. There is no way for me to express how important your efforts have been to me.

I would also like to thank someone I have never met. Like *Cigarettes & Wine*, this novel was written while I was listening to the works of Jason Isbell nonstop, and his records provided a soundtrack for the writing, editing, and revision of the work.

Finally, this novel would not be possible without the years of research I have done on sexualities, gender, religion, and health. I have had the privilege of interviewing and observing so many wonderful bisexual, transgender, non-binary, lesbian, gay, intersex, poly, kink, asexual, and otherwise Queer people formally and informally over the years, and many of their experiences find voice throughout this novel. I would thus like to thank all of them both for sharing their stories with researchers like me, and for being role models to many of us navigating gender, sexualities and relationships throughout contemporary society.

CHAPTER 1

We were supposed to be working the afternoon shift at the coffee shop. We were supposed to be telling each other jokes to pass the time, and maybe arguing over what music should be wafting through the old building with the posters on the walls and the never-quite-clean concrete floors. We were supposed to listen around five in the afternoon as the retired guy explained the merits of chai tea – in excruciating detail, mind you – as he waited for the one he always ordered, or as the white business suit tried to convince us "artsy types" how important the upcoming election was for the nation and why he was working to reelect W for a second term. We were supposed to be annoyed at the rush of incoming and returning college students that seemed to swamp the shop every year throughout the month of August.

We were not, however, supposed to be in Greg's apartment around the corner from the work we skipped out on that day. I don't even think we were supposed to be in Greg's bedroom for any reason now that I think about it, but he was out of town for the weekend and both of us had keys to the place since I crashed there sometimes when I was too tired – or drunk – to make it home at night and Jackson was living there – sleeping on Greg's couch after losing his apartment. I cannot recall exactly why we ended up skipping work – a decision that would cost us both our minimum wage coffee-serving jobs in the end – or how we ended up in Greg's bedroom that day. Maybe it was just the most convenient option because I lived in another part of town. Or maybe there was something comforting about it since the last time I remembered feeling anything for anyone was in another one of Greg's apartments five years before that night. I don't recall how it happened, but in any case, there we were.

In fact, spending that afternoon in bed with Jackson now seems like either the most natural or the most inexplicable outcome possible depending on how I look at it. In the former case, Jackson and I had been flirting with each other, passing notes and jokes at work, and coming within a breath of connecting with each other on a deeper level

© KONINKLIJKE BRILL NV, LEIDEN, 2019 | DOI 10.1163/9789004392212_001

for the entire year he'd been in Atlanta. There was something about him that reminded me of the best parts of my past, and I found myself drawn to him no matter how much I tried to ignore it. He arrived in the summer of 2003 with a backpack and a loose dream of being a writer after finishing college in Texas, losing an important romantic relationship with a guy named River, and needing a change of scenery. It reminded me of running off to Atlanta after losing my first love, and as my friends put it, "kind of treading water somewhere between living and not" for the past five years. We seemed equally lost, but something about that connected us as we spent the next year dancing around the fact that we were both obviously attracted to the other.

While I can look at these things and think of course we finally ended up in bed together, I can just as easily look back on that time in my life and come to the opposite conclusion. At the time, I had become skilled in the art of numbness, and proficient in abstaining from any kind of emotional connection. As silly as it sounds to me now, I thought I had been luckier than most to experience real love with two people already, but I paid a heavy price for that joy when everything changed unexpectedly at the end of high school. I didn't think I wanted to, and didn't know if I could, feel so strongly about anyone or anything again. My response had been to shut down the possibility, avoid intimacy, and adopt a "friends at most only" lifestyle that served me well enough in the years since. I flirted. I danced. I went through the motions with other people, but I didn't let anyone get too close. Though I didn't mean to at the time, I didn't even let the people who had always been closest to me in all that much either during those five years. Until Jackson showed up in my life, this approach seemed to be working well, and I was certain that it was the best way to keep going after what I'd lost.

Of course, as Lena told me so many times even though I wouldn't listen, the problem with this approach was that I was "ignoring all the good" things about my time with her and Jordan by letting my "fear of what could go bad" keep me from trying to find the joy I once had in the first place. She was right. She usually was. It was like the way I would sometimes read a book full of happy memories or beautiful experiences, but lose sight of those things when something terrible happened in the same story. As my shirt hit the floor of Greg's bedroom, taken off by someone else I had real feelings about for the first time in half a decade, I wondered why it was so easy to fixate on the fear and pain even when those moments were drastically outnumbered by the times I felt pleasure, exhilaration, passion, and satisfaction. I didn't know the answer, but somehow Jackson was making me finally start asking the questions.

It started simple enough. I met him on his first day working at the coffee shop in Greg's neighborhood. I had been working there for a while at the time, and I was assigned to train the new guy with the funny accent. I remember Greg thought it was funny that my high school dropout ass got to train the college boy from out west. I thought it was funny too. It also fit into the only real social life I had at the time – collecting stories from strangers. I learned all about his childhood in Louisiana, his college years in Houston, and the love of his life named River. The problem, however, arose when I realized I was starting to care about the answers. It was a sensation I remembered from my younger days, but one that wasn't part of my life anymore. I even felt the old urge – that I shut down and ignored – to run talk to my friends about the interesting guy I met. I think I began to realize I was really in trouble six months after he arrived when he left work with a date, and I felt the first jealous impulse I had in a very long time.

I was shaking. I remember that. I was shaking as he undid my pants, and maybe that should have told me something. Maybe I should have stopped right then, and tried to evaluate the situation or something. Instead, I just figured I was nervous because it had been so long since I was in this position. Even in the moment, I was still trying to tell myself it was no big deal. I was breaking down the barriers that kept me isolated for so long at the same time I was trying to tell myself that I could do this and keep those boundaries in place. It was foolish, in hindsight, but it made sense to me at the time. He kept checking to see if I was okay, probably because of the shaking, and I kept saying I was. I was wrong, but I didn't know that yet. I only realized later that he knew almost nothing about why I didn't date. He knew I wrote stories about a lost love, but he didn't know the details, what it felt like, or any of that.

I'm not even sure I can say now what it felt like. I know the details – the facts of the case as people often say when accidents happen – but the whole experience is a blur for me emotionally even all these years later. I remember feeling like I was drowning all the time. It was hard to breathe. It was hard to think. It was hard to remember I was still alive. I remember I ran to the safest place I knew and did so without really meaning to or knowing what I was doing. I have flashes of memories where I'm almost comatose on the floor by Greg's bed. I have memories of going for late night walks through the neighborhood and knowing that Lena or Greg was walking a few hundred feet behind me just in case without wanting to ever turn around or talk to them about whatever I was thinking on those walks. I remember seeing Jordan's name written in concrete on a sidewalk and having to call Greg for a ride home because I couldn't move. I remember tattooing the same name on my arm in simple black ink. I remember so many details, but I can't remember being able to feel anything.

That was, of course, until one day in February 2004 – right around my birthday – when Jackson was talking about River. River was amazing in every way according to Jackson, but he ultimately left Jackson at the end of college because of Jackson's intimacy issues and difficulty with emotional stuff. I could relate, but even more terrifying in the moment, I felt myself feeling things for some reason. I remember, before that day, thinking I would give anything to feel again, that the numbness was like a disease that covered everything. I remember on that day I realized that the numbness was only a symptom, and the rush of feelings – a combination of limitless pain and joy hitting me all at once – was the real deal. I spent thirty minutes in the bathroom – crying and otherwise releasing fluids – and snuck out of the back of the coffee house as soon as I regained enough composure to do anything but hug the toilet and shake. I wasn't numb anymore, but to my surprise, I really wanted to be numb again if I could.

I avoided Jackson for the next four months. I changed my work schedule, made excuses to leave as soon as he came near me, and even started looking for other jobs. At one point sometime in the spring, he finally cornered me outside of a bar and we just screamed at each other for I don't know how long before going our separate ways. It didn't help. The door was open and the feelings were there. Greg and Lena said it was good because I was starting to finally grieve, but I just wanted to punch them every time they said that kind of stuff. I know they were trying to help, they had been taking care of me for five years after all, but I didn't want help. I wanted to turn it back off. I wanted it to stop. When I woke up on Greg's floor one morning in June after having way too much to drink and crashing there the night before, Jackson was out in the living room. He was moving in after losing his place, and for some reason, I finally gave up and told him what was going on with me.

We spent the summer leading up to that afternoon in August hanging out with the understanding that I didn't want to talk about the past, I wasn't ready to date anyone, and I was an asshole for bailing on him in the spring. As hard as it was, I began intentionally thinking about Jordan, about what Lena and I had back then before we lost him, and how I felt about everything that happened over the years. I also started talking, though I really didn't want to, about these things with Lena and Greg. At their request, though if possible even less welcome in my mind at the time, I even reached out and began talking about these things with Abs and Claire and visiting both when I could. They'd both been patient with my silence over the years, but like any real friends I can imagine, they were also quick to point out how painful and horrible my disappearing acts had been for them.

The conversations helped, to my surprise, and I started to feel like myself again, well, at least a little bit. I wasn't the same me I had been as a teenager, but Abs pointed out that I probably never would be the same me again. "Some things change us on such a deep level that there is no going back," she said one day while her girlfriend Lisa helped us pack for her move to graduate school in Florida. "You just, you know, you become a new you that kind of blends what you were with who you are now as you experience different things." Considering the ways college had changed her, the logic made sense to me, but the reality was difficult to reconcile. I kept having the conversations and thinking about all these things, but for some reason, I never discussed any of this with Jackson, and I still wonder if that played a role in the way things went that afternoon in Greg's bedroom.

In some ways, I could not have asked for a better re-introduction to emotion than what I got from Jackson. He was kind, gentle, and talented with his body in ways that still make me smile all these years later. He was understanding and careful with me in a way that I'm sure was tied to the fact that he knew beforehand that I was going through a lot. He took care of me like a long-time lover, and our embrace felt right, honest, and free. Even though I would intentionally never see him again after that night, I still think I might have made something special with him at another time in my life. Instead, I lost all composure and any semblance of numbness that night as I finished our time together in that bedroom curled in a fetal position sobbing and repeatedly whispering Jordan's name.

CHAPTER 2

"You had sex with someone you like," Lena says unable to hide her shock. She came home to find me sitting on the floor of our kitchen writing in a notebook, and instead of saying hello, I told her how I spent the afternoon. I laughed as she dropped her shopping bags right as she spoke those words and sat down on the floor in front of me. She took my hand, and said, "Are you okay, silly?"

"I don't know," I said shaking my head. "I feel a little bit like our groceries," I added pointing to the bags scattered on the floor in a mess.

"I would think so," she said laughing and shaking her head. For the first time in years, I found myself aware of the eyes of the woman I loved more than any woman I'd ever known in my life. Lena and Jordan were my twin first loves, best friends alongside Abs and later Claire, and heroes growing up, but something shifted when we lost Jordan. I stopped talking to Abs almost completely until she showed up at the apartment I shared with Greg and Lena back then and read me the riot act for abandoning her. We were only now starting to talk regularly again, but I did make sure never to completely disappear again after that interaction. Looking back, I think the problem was that I could never hide anything from Abs, she wouldn't let me, and during that time I kind of just wanted to hide from everyone and everything in the world.

"I didn't expect it to be like this," I said softly, choking up a little bit, "I don't know what I feel right now, or I guess, what I should feel, I don't know." She rubs my hand with smooth, soft motions like she did when I was just a little kid living down the road who got scared of this or that movie I watched without my parents' permission. It hits me that I've really missed her even though we've been living together for five years, first in her and Greg's place and then here in our apartment in College Park. I start crying and lean forward until my head lands on her shoulder. It also hits me that this is the most physical contact I've had with her since I practically lived in her and Greg's laps throughout

© KONINKLIJKE BRILL NV, LEIDEN, 2019 | DOI 10.1163/9789004392212_002

the year after we lost Jordan. She runs her fingers through my hair the way she used to when we were kids and then teens, the way she did that terrible year, and I feel her choking up too.

"I've missed you silly," she says with a shaky voice.

"I'm sorry," I say, and then I just keep saying it. After about the ninth time, I get quiet again, and then add, "I'm so sorry, I just couldn't…"

"I know," she says in the same shaky voice, "You didn't do anything wrong Kid." Even in that moment, it struck me that Lena was the only person who sounded strange when using my preferred name. She said, "It wasn't your fault, it was an accident and you couldn't have stopped it." We've had this exchange before, often in the middle of the night when I'd been drinking too much, but this time it feels more real. We stay on the floor together for a long time without saying anything.

A while, I honestly don't remember how long, later, we make a couple glasses of wine, and step out on the porch together. She calls Lucy to see if it's okay to reschedule their date so she can stay and chat with me. Lucy laughs so loud I hear her through the phone and explains that she is knee-deep in her latest masterpiece and was about to make a similar call. They agree to get together the next day after Lucy's doctor's appointment for a bite to eat. When she puts down the phone, she says, "So, do you want to tell me about it?"

"Yeah," I say remembering the days where I told Lena and Abs everything that happened in my life no matter how minor, "I think that would be good."

"Well, I remember how to listen," she says with a laugh.

"I deserve that," I say laughing along with her. "It was strange, you know, it was wonderful honestly, but then I lost it and ended up crying like a baby for about an hour. It freaked me out Lena, and I'm pretty sure it freaked Jackson out too."

"Jackson?"

"Yeah."

"The goofy wannabe writer that works with you at the shop?"

"Yeah, so?"

"It's just not who I would have expected, I mean, I know you had a crush on him and all that, but I don't know, I didn't see you and him actually doing anything."

"Well, we won't be again."

"Why not?"

"I don't know, I feel like being with him would be too intense for me right now, I don't know if that makes sense, but I don't really want to see him again, maybe ever, but at least not anytime soon." I still don't know why I felt this way, but I think there was a part of me that saw a future when I looked at Jackson, and I was barely able to contemplate the present and the past much less a future at that point.

"Do you think it was the crying thing," she asks taking a sip of her pinot, "Because, I mean, I think that would be easy to understand if you told him about Jordan and the last few years and all that, I mean, I'm not surprised at all that you got overwhelmed the first time you had sex, I mean that kind of sex, again."

"Really?"

"Well," she says lighting a cigarette, and handing me one when I motion for it. "Yeah, I mean, the last time you had sex that meant something you were a completely different person, and it was with Jordan, I mean, come on, did you really think you could just jump back on the horse, even years later, like it was nothing?"

"I don't think I really thought about it at all."

"Then think about it silly," she says taking a puff. "You lost the most significant relationship of your life without any warning. It hurt so much that you could barely look at – much less touch or be with – your other first love," she says this while posing in her favorite posture for photographs, "And even now, I don't know if you can even see me that way anymore because of how intertwined our relationship always was with you and Jordan." I nod, and for the first time, I realize that I don't see her the same way I used to, and I don't feel the same desires. She feels more like Abs always has to me these days, but I never noticed the shift. "And on top of that, it hurt so much that you completely abandoned and hid from your best friends – other than me – because that was the only way you would feel safe from getting hurt like that again." She smiles at me and taps my hand, "I don't think there was any chance you could have been intimate with anyone again without it being overwhelming at first."

"Why didn't I run away from you, I mean, I get what you're saying, but wouldn't I have hidden from you too if you're right?"

"I don't think you can run from me silly – I think our relationship is different than any of the others, like your relationship with Jordan was different from any other, even different from what we have."

"What do you mean?"

"We're each other's safe spaces silly," she says laughing. "Think about it, before we were ever friends or lovers, before we loved each other like we did then and like we do now and like we probably always will, I was the one who protected you when you were a little kid scared of your own shadow. You were the silly little kid that I wanted to steal or adopt as my own. We've always come running to each other whenever we were in trouble, the same way you and Jordan were always a couple and never "just" friends even when things were hard, the same ways Abs has always been your best friend even when one or both of you abandoned the other or disappeared for some reason. You and I are just linked to each other, I don't know why. You're where I always feel safe, and I'm that for you no matter what else we might be at the time."

"So, when I needed safety more than ever before, I ran to you."

"Yep."

"But," I say trying to figure this out, "Then what happened to you and me, you know, like we were back then, I mean…"

"As lovers?"

"Yeah."

"I don't think that was possible then because I don't think we can be together like that without feelings, and you were trying like hell not to feel anything." She sips her wine and finishes her cigarette. "I think you came looking for your childhood hero, and I saw my scared little silly from back then so we just kind of shifted again."

"Do you think we'll shift back again at some point?"

Laughing, she says, "I have no clue, but I don't think it really matters since I can't imagine us not being in each other's lives somehow."

"Same here, but I do wonder about it."

"Me too."

"So, what do I do with all these feelings?" I watch as she lights another smoke, and finish my own glass of wine. I ask if she wants another, and after she says yes, I go grab two more from the kitchen. When I come back, I light another smoke. "Remember when we used to do this all the time, I mean, just talk out on porches?"

"Yeah," she says laughing, "It's nice to do it again."

"It is."

"About the feelings," she says then pauses waiting for me to nod. "I think you just have to let yourself feel them like you have been the past couple months. I think that's it, I mean, even more so tonight, but lately you've seemed more like yourself again, I mean, this may sound crazy, but," she laughs and taps an ash from her cigarette, "It's almost like you're coming back to life or waking up from a hibernation or something lately."

"It doesn't sound crazy," I say smiling and imagining myself as a bear wandering out of a cave and back into the forest. "It kind of feels like that for me too."

"I guess you, or really we, just go with it, I mean, that's what Lucy said I should do when you showed up wanting to actually talk with us instead of disappearing into your room back in June. She said it was like her mom after her dad passed away, one day she just kind of started coming back a little at a time, and she thinks that's what you're doing."

"Have I ever mentioned that I like Lucy, and that I'm very happy for the two of you?"

"Nope."

"I've kind of been an asshole, haven't I?"

"Yep."

"I'm sorry."

"You're forgiven, and honestly, you haven't been terrible. You just didn't want anything to do with anything, it was more like you were rude or absent than anything else. Lucy said her mom was like that too for a few years so maybe it's a normal part of grief or something."

"I'm still sorry, and I'll tell Lucy that too."

"You should, she's pretty great."

Pointing at the big grin on her face, I say, "Yeah, that much I could tell." She laughs and blushes the way she often does when Lucy is around. I realize I've spent very little time around the two of them together, and I make plans to change that. "Hey Lena?"

"Yeah?"

"Does it make any sense that, like when I was crying earlier and even now, that I kind of feel like I cheated on Jordan, and maybe even you today? I know that's not true, you know, but it kind of feels like it for some reason."

"I think it makes sense," she says looking out into the sky for a moment. "Abs suggested something like that from one of the books she read in college, something about how spousal relationships – and I guess others, but the book was talking about spouses – don't necessarily end when a person dies because they often continue in some way, even for the rest of your life, for the person or people left behind. So, Abs' book would say that, for you, the relationship with Jordan – and even with me to some extent – from back then is not over and you might feel that way as you adjust what those relationships mean in your life now." She laughs, "Soon-to-be Dr. Abs could say it better, but does that make sense or seem right?"

"Yeah," I say thinking about it for a minute, "Yeah, I think that makes sense, I mean, as weird as it is even for me, I kind of still feel like no time has passed, you know, like right now, right here, it's still that day I passed out in your doorway right after everything happened, and I've felt that way all summer, I mean, like I'm just now starting to deal with it, I guess."

"I think that's exactly what's happening."

"But that was five years ago?"

"But maybe you needed some time before you could face it and start over."

"I guess."

Lena nods, and we keep talking for a long time. We stay up all night, moving back and forth from the porch to the couch to grabbing some takeout at the restaurant of a nearby hotel at one point. We spend more time like this, like we used to, in the coming weeks and months, and she is the one that tells me about Jackson leaving town in September. We also hang out with Lucy and Greg a lot more than I had before, and I keep thinking about Jordan, about the passage of time, and about what I might want to do with my life. The pain doesn't go away, but it does feel like I'm making progress and handling it better as the days go by. I still think I see Jordan sometimes on this sidewalk or at that train stop, but without even realizing it at the time, I stop having what I would call panic attacks every time it happens. Instead, I start wondering what happens after people die, and where, if anywhere, he might be. I wonder if he sees me, if he remembers me, and even if he would be disappointed in me for wasting five years hiding from my life or maybe proud of me for beginning to try to live again now. I don't know what might be coming next, but I begin, for the first time since I was a teenager, to want to find out.

CHAPTER 3

"What's up doc," I say as I see Abs come bouncing down the aisle from the terminals in the Atlanta airport.

"Wow," she says giggling, "I didn't even know you could still do that Kid."

"Do what?"

"Smile," she shouts and grabs me an intense – and incredibly powerful – full-body hug. Giggling, she says, "I haven't seen you smiling in so long, and it's the perfect way to start Thanksgiving break."

"That's not true, is it," I ask genuinely curious.

Nodding her head, she says, "It is, and remember, I'm still always right."

"Well," I say joining her giggle, "You are becoming a doctor."

"Duh," she says laughing harder and finally releasing me, "I'm awesome."

"You sure are," I say, and we start walking toward the exit that leads to the MARTA. She is, as is customary, swinging her Winnie the Pooh bag as we walk arm-in-arm through the airport. I'm amazed the damn thing still hasn't fallen apart, though I do notice that it has some more new stitching in places. She's wearing a novelty t-shirt with a Palmetto Rose on it that reminds me of her parents' – ongoing as of Thanksgiving 2004 – search for the perfect one of those things. I remember the way they showed up like clockwork in our neighborhood as we aged, and the joy we got teasing Jordan because he was the only one of us that liked the damn things. "Especially with that shirt," I say laughing as we reach the exit doors and leave the main part of the airport.

"Don't you love it, like so much," she asks in an excited tone, "I found it when Lisa and I went to Charleston last year, and I just had to have it."

"I'm sure your parents are proud."

"Yes, it was the one thing missing from my daughter resume," she says using her hands to mime ticking things off a checklist.

© KONINKLIJKE BRILL NV, LEIDEN, 2019 | DOI 10.1163/9789004392212_003

"How is Lisa?"

At this point, we stop dead in our tracks because Abs starts laughing so hard that she has to bend over and hold her stomach for a few minutes. I have no clue what is going on, but she is saying hold on repeatedly, and from the sound of it, gasping for breath at the funniest thing she has ever heard or seen. She moves her hands to her face and continues to laugh. I don't know what I did, but I start laughing too because her reaction is hilarious. After a few minutes, and about twelve recitations of hold on, she finally says, "Okay, I'm sorry, okay," but she starts laughing again and moves over to the wall, leans against it, and wipes her eyes.

"What did I do," I finally ask because I can't take it anymore.

"Nothing," she says starting to regain her normal voice, "It's just, you know, too perfect that the first time you ask about her is after we stop dating." She starts laughing again, and I admit it is kind of funny. They've been together, or were together I guess, through most of college, and though I didn't realize it, I had never asked about the relationship. It was another example of just how checked out I had been in the past few years. "She's fine," Abs says after a few more minutes, "She decided to take a year off instead of starting the MFA program down in central Florida and is living in some small town near here working at a café and studying Flannery O'Connor. I don't understand it, you know, but she's really happy there."

"What happened with y'all?"

"Nothing major," she says smiling, "We love each other, but we decided to take a break since grad school is about all I have time for right now, the first semester has been just as intense as everyone said it would be, and we're not sure we want the same things in the future, you know, so while she's kind of finding herself and I'm getting used to grad school, we're just taking some time off and we'll see if we fit together later, you know."

"How do you feel about that?"

"Look at you asking questions like a real person again."

"I know, I know, but really, how do you feel?"

"I feel great, you know, and so does she. I don't think either of us have ever loved someone the way we love each other, you know,

I don't want to send you back into hermit mode, but I think, for me, she is kind of like the level you and Jordan had, you know."

"It's okay to talk about him Abs."

"Well," she says smiling, "I'll have to get used to that again."

"I know, and I love you for everything, okay?"

"I love you too, but yeah, Lisa is like that for me, I love her so much, and part of that is she needs to figure out what she wants, and let's face it, she can afford to take time off and do that kind of thing, you know, so I think this is good, you know, we'll see where it goes, like on our own terms, our way, and we'll still see each other and stuff when we want to."

"Makes sense to me, what's the future issue, I mean, what's that about?"

"You remember how Jordan loved the small town thing, and you did not?"

"Yep," I say and surprise myself by smiling at the memory. That is starting to happen occasionally, I smile when I think about him instead of feeling only pain, or only a mixture of happy and sad at the same time. I hope it continues.

"Same thing," she says as we enter the station, and move down to the platform where the trains come in and go out every few minutes. Lena and I live at the first stop after the airport so the ride will be short, and Abs is staying with us for the holiday. "She loves that stuff, she talked about how amazing Rock Hill was the whole time we were in school, but I don't know about all that, you know, I liked being so close to Charlotte, and though it's not a huge city, I like Tallahassee now and I think I'd like to land here or maybe in Tampa or Orlando down in central Florida, you know, so we'll have to figure out that kind of stuff, you know, nothing major, just kind of life planning types of things that will matter at some point. Right now, we're both young and we have things we want to do, you know, like her with the Flannery O'Connor pilgrimage and me with grad school, so we're just giving each other freedom to do our own thing, and we'll see where it goes, you know, that kind of thing."

"You are so together."

"And you're a damn mess."

17

"Pretty much."

"What about you, have you dipped your toes into having a love life again?"

"Not really," I say smiling and blushing for some reason, "I had a date, but all it told me was that I am not ready for that yet."

"What happened?"

"Nothing really, I mean, nothing like with Jackson or anything, I didn't freak out again, I mean, but it was just strange and awkward."

"Maybe it was the person?"

"I don't think so, she was great, I mean, really great. She works with Lucy, well, kind of, she manages one of the galleries Lucy sometimes shows her work in, and she scared me so I don't think it was anything to do with her."

"Scared you?"

"Yeah, like Jackson did, like I liked her, she was fun."

"Oh," she says laughing, "Okay, I know what you mean, and yeah, if you felt something for her then you're probably right, but hey, who knows, you probably just need some time and maybe to meet the right person, you know, I'm kind of impressed you went on a date."

Laughing, I say, "Yeah, that's what Lena said, but I don't know, ever since starting to, what did you call it, try again and talk to people, I don't know, I really like and trust Lucy so when Lucy mentioned this woman, I thought, why not, I mean, Lucy told her my situation and she was cool with that, you know, the bi stuff, the grieving stuff, the non-binary stuff, so I thought why not give it a shot."

Abs hugs me without warning, and softly says, "And that sounds like the old you."

"Yeah," I say with my arms around her, "I'm trying."

As our bodies part, the train arrives. We walk in and grab seats together. She turns in her seat, and asks, "I have a question for you about Lucy."

"What's up?"

"Well, you know, I've only met her once, but I get the impression that Lena is serious about her, right?"

"Oh yeah," I say smiling, "Lena is in love and so is Lucy."

"Okay," Abs says smiling, "So, then, I need some advice before we all hang out."

"About what?"

"The medical stuff," she says, "I mean, do we talk about it, is it off limits, what does Lucy prefer, you know, because I don't want to be an asshole accidentally."

"Only intentional assholery for Abs, got it."

"Shut up," she says laughing.

"No," I say laughing, "It's a good question, I didn't even think about it because of the way Lucy treats the subject. She is just open about it, and talks about it, answers questions about it, you name it, no problem, so just be your normal self and it'll be cool."

"Oh cool," Abs says smiling, "That's easy, and that's how it is at school, but, you know, I wanted to do whatever Lucy prefers because she's the one who lives with it, you know."

"Oh yeah," I say, "That's the same approach I take, and honestly what Lucy would suggest if, like me, you asked for her advice." It only takes a few minutes, and we arrive at the College Park station, and depart the train. "Lucy just loves who she is, I mean, she is just like 'I am Lucy, I have CF and I'm a lesbian, I'm still alive, hear me ROAR,' you know, she just embraces who and how she is, and everyone else around her better do the same or else because she won't take shit from, well, from anyone."

"I'm going to like her."

"Yes, you are," I say as we cross the railroad tracks, and head into mine and Lena's neighborhood. Abs is in town for the entire weekend, and Lucy has an art show on Friday night at a gallery in Decatur. The four of us spend the time together roaming around the city like a bunch of goofy kids, and as Abs and Lena both note before the end of the holiday weekend, it almost feels like we went back to the nineties for a little while. On Sunday, a few hours before Abs flies back to Florida, Lisa drives into town, and the three of us have an amazing brunch before spending hours poring over records at a shop in Little Five. Almost as if Jordan planned it that way, Abs finds a copy of his favorite Whitney Houston album on vinyl, and I spend the night listening to it in my bedroom after saying goodbye to Abs and Lisa at the airport.

CHAPTER 4

"Do you realize you keep humming the same song every few minutes or so," I ask looking through a rack of skirts in the back corner of a thrift store not far from another coffee shop I used to work at and next door to the theatre Lucy got me a job at after Thanksgiving. It's early spring, and I've just realized that somewhere along the way I started only wearing my skirts, makeup, and other "women's" clothes at home, when I was out of town, or after I was already drunk. I don't know when or how that started, but I guess part of getting myself back, whatever version that will be this time, involves reclaiming at least as much of the freedom I felt with my visual gender fluidity – and clothing tastes – as I had gained by the end of high school.

"Huh," Greg says turning from the rack of shirts he's inspecting, "No, I, I didn't notice. Is it bothering you?"

"Nope, I just wondered what song it was," I say finding an orange pleated skirt with tiny off-white swirls on the left leg. I like this, I think, and feel myself choke up a little bit – a feeling I'm getting used to, though having less and less over time – as I decide to try it on.

"Oh," Greg says holding up two different shirts in the light, shaking his head, and putting them back. "It's an old song from when I was a kid, I've just had it stuck in my head for a while." He keeps looking through the shirts as I go into one of the dressing rooms, shake a bit more than I would like, take a deep breath, look in every direction like I did when I was a kid looking at "women's" magazines in a shop near my house, and finally try on the damn skirt. I step out of the dressing room, walking slower than normal, and say, "What do you think mate?" Personally, I think it's perfect.

Greg smiles, and says, "Ooh, I think it works for you," as he smiles and comes over to take a look. "Now, if I could only find a halfway decent shirt, we'd be set."

"What's up with you Greg," I say trying to remember any time where he had issues with clothes. I mean, we jokingly call him

© KONINKLIJKE BRILL NV, LEIDEN, 2019 | DOI 10.1163/9789004392212_004

Mr. Fashion sometimes because he is the only person any of us have ever met that can literally find a way to make anything look good. Repeatedly humming the same song, having issues finding clothes, something is up and now I want to know what. "It's not like you to have any issue finding clothes?" I go back into the dressing room to get my stuff, but I decide I'm going to wear the skirt right away.

"What," he says in an unconvincing tone, "I don't know what you mean."

"Yeah you do, what's up mate?"

"It's not important, no big deal," he says, which as Lena and I know is Greg code for anything important. I just stare at him for a few minutes until he says, "Finally," let's out a deep breath, and asks, "You ready to check out," while holding up a beautiful soft green button-down dress shirt that I think – even with my limited fashion abilities – will go well with a tie he loves.

"Okay," I say as we move toward the back of the store where the registers are located, "But when you're ready, I'm happy to listen to whatever is up with you."

We buy the clothes, and head out into the neighborhood. There is a café that serves noodle dishes nearby, and Greg promised me lunch if I would go shopping with him. As we walk through the neighborhood, he starts humming the same song again, and I start laughing. "What," he says smiling and swinging the bag with his new shirt and my old pants in his hand.

Shaking my head, I say, "You're humming the song again." He nods but doesn't say anything. We arrive at the restaurant and take seats outside at the same table we always sit at.

We order without any need for menus, and after the waiter leaves, he says, "Look, it's no big deal, or at least not yet, I just think I met someone cool, that's all."

"So, what, you're humming a love song?"

"Not exactly," he says laughing and blushing just enough to tell me he really likes whoever this new person is. "It's an old Counting Crows song called "Sullivan Street," but I honestly have no clue what the song is about."

"I remember that song," I say, "I think Abs had that tape. I think it was one of the ones she played on repeat all the damn time when we were in middle school. Why are you humming it all the time?" I did remember the song, but I was almost certain it wasn't much of a love song in any kind of way that I could recall. I memorized every song on that tape because Abs was head-over-heels in love with it for at least a year, and still considered it one of her favorites for some reason I never understood no matter how many times I heard it.

"Remember when I went to that Gospel thing at that gay bar," he asks as our drinks arrive, and the waiter disappears again.

"Yeah, what about it?"

"Well," he says and blushes again, "I met this guy named Sullivan, he was there with another guy, David I think, anyway, I don't know, I liked him, I mean, I like him, a lot."

Laughing, I say, "Okay, the song makes more sense now."

Chuckling even louder than I am, he says, "Well, it actually fits even better than you think," and smiles in a way that makes his eyes kind of shine.

"Do tell?"

"His last name is Street," he says starting to laugh again, "Can you believe that shit?"

"You're making that up," I say almost choking on my water at the thought.

"I'm not, I promise you."

"That's just too perfect," I say still half-expecting to later learn that he is full of shit. Instead of saying so, though, I ask, "So, what's he like?"

"Well," Greg says, "It's a little odd for me because he's a preacher, or well, he's becoming a preacher, he's in Bible school over in South Carolina, but comes here a lot because he's from a small town in South Georgia."

"Okay, a gay preacher, I can dig that, how do you feel about it?"

"Well, he's not gay either."

"Please say he's bi because we both know how chasing straights goes," I say chuckling as our big bowls of noodles arrive. The waiter asks if we need anything else, we say no, and he disappears again as we both begin to eat.

"I'm not chasing straights, never again after last time," he says and we both start laughing. He was crazy about some banker in Midtown a couple years back, and it was the ultimate shit show. The guy, bless his heart as they would say where I grew up, drove Greg nuts for about four months before having his own straight preacher call to tell Greg to stop corrupting his parishioners. "He's bi, like you and Lena and Abs and out about it too except at work, I checked," he says between bites and bursts of laughter, "Never again, I tell you, never again."

"Okay," I say regaining my composure, "Well, I guess same thing, bi preacher, I can dig that and like the gay ones, probably plenty of bi ones too, I guess."

"Yeah, that's what I guess too," he says and we both do some eating for a few minutes before he adds, "I'm not sure about the religion thing though."

"I can understand that, what kind of religious person is he," I ask thinking about the varieties I've seen so far in my life, especially related to people like us.

"A strange one."

"Strange, how?"

"He's an agnostic Christian is how he puts it."

"Okay," I say with a laugh, "What is that?"

"He believes in some kind of higher power, and the teachings of Jesus, stuff like that, but he's not sure there is anything up there, and doesn't think people should push their beliefs on other people, does that make sense?"

"I guess so," I say thinking back to my teen years, "It doesn't sound that different from what Daniel and Roger believed, or Jordan for that matter." I silently congratulate myself for the latest time I've said Jordan's name in conversation without any problems, and then I smile remembering all the times I listened as he talked about his faith.

"That's what I was wondering about, like, was it hard being with someone who had beliefs, like, you didn't believe any of that stuff, right?"

"Right, not even a little bit."

"So, was that hard for y'all?"

I thought about it for a second, and said, "No, not really. I mean, we had our issues, but never about his faith. Like, we had issues with churches and with some of the people at the gay church he went to later, but his faith was never an issue. He would talk about what he believed, and I would talk about what I thought, and I don't know, it was kind of nice, like a hobby he had that I didn't have, at least for me. It might have been harder for him, at times, that I didn't believe any of it, but nothing, best I can remember, all that big of a deal I don't think."

"Really?"

"Yeah, best I can remember, yeah, it wasn't a big deal. He had beliefs I didn't, but I had opinions he didn't, you know? It was just something we talked about a lot."

"That makes me feel better, I guess," he says smiling again like he was earlier. "And didn't you say, a while back I swear I remember this, that you knew a religious gay couple that were, like, doing well and happy with religion and everything."

"I'm honestly surprised you don't know any Greg," I said laughing, "I mean, you do love those gospel night things."

Laughing, he says, "Yeah, you know what, I probably do, but I don't really ever talk about religion with anyone now that I think about it."

"That makes sense, I don't either, I mean, what do I care since I'm not a believer, you know?"

"Exactly."

"But yeah, if it helps, I know a few, and hell, Roger and Daniel were together forever mate. But even some I grew up with, like Lenny and What's His Name out in Tennessee, that was just what fit for them and once they got past bullshit straight definitions of religion, they did fine and built great lives together. So, I don't know, but I don't think it matters if they're not in the hateful groups or what not, you know."

"That's what I was thinking because this guy is awesome, but I just don't know what to do with the religion stuff. I mean, you're right, I like going to churches and to the events at the bars and that kind of thing, but I don't know much about the beliefs side of it."

"You probably don't need to," I say smiling and thinking about Jordan again, "He'll probably tell you anything you need to know about his beliefs."

"Yeah," he says smiling again, "I guess I just like this one a lot, like, a whole lot, and so I'm trying to think of everything that could go wrong like I always do."

"I'm with you there these days mate, but what is it you keep telling me, you got to give it a shot if you ever hope to get anything worthwhile, tell yourself that."

"You know, it doesn't work as well when I tell myself that."

"I get that too," I say, and we share a laugh as the people move from store to store on the sidewalks around us.

CHAPTER 5

The summer of 2005 found me on the road. It had been almost a year since my afternoon with Jackson, and over a year since I started talking about and feeling things again. I had even been on a few dates by that point, but I still didn't seem ready for anything romantic. Or maybe I just still needed to find the "next right person," as Lena put it. I spent my time reading, writing in my journals, and working at the theatre taking tickets, cleaning up, and helping with the plays and other events. I had enough money set aside for a nice, short vacation, or a chance to just roam around for a while on the cheap. After talking with Lena for hours about it, I decided to try out some new places, and Lucy's roommate let me rent or borrow her beat up Chevy pickup truck if I promised to write her some of my, as she put it, "sappy meets morose poetry" that she could turn into songs for her band.

The first thing I did was head south along I-75. From what I could tell, a few hours would find me in the city where Abs was becoming a doctor, and I thought she might enjoy a surprise visit in the middle of her summer classes. She was living on the second floor of an old house that had been converted into apartments in a part of Tallahassee called midtown, and I found it, sitting between dogwood trees on 7th Avenue, without much trouble. Her roommate said she was a few blocks away at a café on something called Lake Ella, and a few minutes later I found the café, and a bunch of birds roaming around the human-made lake. I walked up to a familiar stack of books, tapped Abs on the shoulder, and said, "Is this seat taken?"

"OH MY GOD," she screamed, and I think I scared some of the birds. "What are you doing here?"

"Finally couldn't put up with Lena anymore."

"It was only a matter of time," she said as we shared laughs and hugs. "Really, what are you doing down here?"

"I decided to do some exploring over the summer."

© KONINKLIJKE BRILL NV, LEIDEN, 2019 | DOI 10.1163/9789004392212_005

"You missed me that much," she said as I sat down across from her and took a sip of my own coffee.

"Of course," I said and watched people walking around the lake in twos, threes, and sometimes by themselves. The birds kind of followed them and ran away from them at the same time. There were a group of people playing with a dog right in front of the porch where we sat, and a cool, short breeze floated across the water toward us for a few moments. "But I don't want to get in the way of your studies so I'll disappear quick if you want."

Smiling, she says, "Nah, you're good, just reading up on teaching strategies for this summer course we all have to take as part of the program. We're about halfway into it so I do have class every day, but I welcome the company if you want to stay for a while."

"How about a night?"

"As long as we make it a night to remember."

"Naturally."

"Wonderful," she says laughing. We spent the next couple hours chatting about Tallahassee before walking around the lake, and then parting ways as she walked back to her house and I picked up the truck before I forgot about it. After showing me her, to my eyes massive, apartment, we went to a place on the corner of Monroe and 4th Avenue to get some Decent pizza slices, and then headed down to the Florida State campus to take a walk. I wanted to see where she went to school, and she wanted to show me the same. We strolled down the pathways on the campus, and marveled at all the beautiful buildings, dogwood trees, and banners advertising this or that degree program, event, or school slogan. When we arrived in front of an ugly looking building with the name Bellamy written on it, she grabbed a seat on a concrete shelf, lit a cigarette, and said, "This is my home for the next few years."

"Why aren't you in one of the pretty buildings," I asked laughing.

"Because the nice buildings all go to the football team and the conservative donors."

"Naturally," I said. "I thought you college folk were all about the liberal utopia type stuff and indoctrinating the youth," I added in my best overly southern accent.

"Spoken like a person that has never actually been to college."

"Hey," I said laughing, "I've been to a few basketball games, and even slept on the floor of a dorm room, thank you very much."

"That was my room fool," she says and sticks her tongue out at me.

Just then, an – and I'm not just saying this because it was a college campus, it was true – absentminded looking person wearing ugly, multi-colored shorts came out the front door. Spotting Abs, they said, "Hey," and she waved back to them. They stopped beside us, nodded at me while somehow appearing afraid of me at the same time, and said, "Have you done your guest lecture yet Abs?" Abs would tell me their name later, but I forget what it was. I spent the whole interaction wondering if they knew how ugly those shorts were.

"Nope," she said smiling, "I do mine at the end of the week, why?"

"I don't know, I just did mine, okay, and I think I did fine, but there was this one kid, Roy Lee something or other, that had like twelve questions I didn't know the answer to so now I'm sure that Dr. Pina is going to think I'm an idiot or something."

"You worry too much," Abs said laughing, "Did you handle the questions well?"

"Yeah, I mean, I think so, and the student came by and said thanks after class so I guess it wasn't so bad, I just, I don't know, I wasn't ready for an undergrad to stump me in front of my boss, you know?"

"I'm sure you'll be fine," Abs said, and after they whined a few more minutes, the absentminded looking person left us alone and disappeared into the scenery of the campus. "They really do worry way too much," Abs said after they were gone.

"What was that about?"

"For practice, we have to go into a classroom and give a lecture to the students on some topic – I'm doing mine on the history of women's movements."

"You have to do that in your first year?"

"Yep, but it's no big deal."

"Speak for yourself Abs, I think I'd be even more nervous than your buddy."

"Whatever," she says laughing, "I want coffee." With that, we walked back to the car, and Abs directed us to a coffee shop that looked like a hippy commune on Railroad Avenue. We drank coffee and laughed together for hours before going back to her house. That night, I slept on the couch in the living room that felt like it was at least as big as mine and Lena's apartment, and the next morning, I woke up to a note from Abs. She was at school and would be gone most of the day. Her note said I was welcome to stay as long as I wanted, but I already felt the pull of the road. I sat on the porch outside the front of the house her apartment was in for two hours writing her a long note and composing a fresh poem about Tallahassee for Lucy's roommate. After I finished, I drove up a road called Thomasville, the same one I came in on, and took the exit for Interstate 10 heading east toward Jacksonville.

I didn't really know where I was going when I left that day. The only plan I had when I left Atlanta was to go see Abs for a day or two. With that finished, I drove past the series of small towns – like Live Oak, Lake City, and Madison – listed on the exits with my cigarettes diminishing and my CD's blaring from the truck's old stereo. I reached Jacksonville a couple hours later, but I did not feel like stopping so I merged onto I-95 and headed north. As I drove, I started thinking about how much fun it would have been to tell Jordan about all the places I was seeing, passing, and maybe even staying in for a night or two on this trip. I began talking to the other side of the front seat as if he was there with me, and when I reached Brunswick, Georgia, I stopped at a Waffle House, ate some grits, and wrote a letter to Jordan.

As I got back on the interstate, I felt kind of silly. I wrote this letter about my day, and then I left it in the bathroom as if Jordan would come by someday and see it. I didn't know why I did it, but somehow, it felt good. It felt like a release, or maybe some kind of therapeutic kind of thing. I felt silly, but I decided to keep doing it. It couldn't do any harm to write him letters, and maybe, if I got the kind of release that first one gave me, maybe it would help. Maybe it would be a way to stay in touch with him and move on at the same time. I thought about this the rest of the day, and by the time I paid for a cheap motel room at a Super 8 in Charleston, South Carolina, I wanted to make the letter writing a regular part of the trip.

I don't think it was a coincidence that I stopped in Charleston instead of somewhere else along the route. I was headed north without any real destination in mind, but Charleston seemed to call my name. I was thinking about going there with Abs when we were kids and wondering if I could find a good book about Palmetto Roses to send back to her in Florida. After I put all my stuff away that night, I wrote Jordan another letter about my trip – this one explaining my plans to pick up a souvenir for Abs while I was in Charleston. Once again, I felt more peaceful after writing and then throwing away the letter – I left this one in a gas station across the street from the motel. I didn't know what to make of this at the time, and I'm not sure if I do now, but it felt good. I had a cigarette after getting rid of the letter, and then I slept for most of the next day – aside from waking up to renew the room.

I ended up spending over three weeks in Charleston. I didn't plan to be there more than a few days, but I became captivated by the market area of town. I would wake up in the morning, have some coffee from the pot in the Super 8 lobby, and head downtown. I would spend the day roaming around, looking in the shops that all seemed to sell things no one could really need, and writing – poetry for Lucy's roommate and other things – at a café that seemed to only own Lucinda Williams' CDs. The second week I was there I sent Abs an "Illustrated Guide to Palmetto Roses" and the third week I was there I spent two hours on the phone with Lena talking about my letter writing and the freedom of being away for a while. She thought it sounded like something beyond or maybe more than just freedom, like a chance to reflect and think without anything else in the world to worry about. I could tell she was jealous, and I liked that.

Like the rest of the trip, I didn't plan to leave Charleston on the morning I did. Instead, I simply woke up and went about what had become my normal routine. When it was time to renew the room, however, I just didn't. Rather, I went out to the beat up, red Chevy-S10, and hit the road headed north. Ten hours later I parked at a cheap – it said economy on the sign – motel just outside of Washington, D.C., and went to sleep after writing Jordan another letter. The next day, I visited all the tourist spots in D.C. – like Jordan always said he would – to see if there was anything special about them. There was not, at least from what I could tell, but I did find a great coffee shop at one of the train stops where I spent most of the evening talking to the locals. That night, I slept at the economy motel again, but around five in the morning the sound of gun shots coming from nearby woke me up, and I once again headed north unsure of where I was going.

This was how I found myself going to sleep in a terribly disgusting SRO in Manhattan on the first night in July. The place was horrid, but I found reasonable parking nearby, it was situated right above an Asian market that had fresh food and other things each day, and it was near a subway stop – about six blocks – so it would do. To get into the place, you had to walk up this long, narrow flight of stairs that always seemed to reverberate with the sounds coming from the walls on either side. The bathroom was a shared space that looked like it might not have been cleaned in the past decade, and the room had just barely more space than the truck I was driving with the added bonus of a small television that hung over the bed and seemed to be threatening to fall on my head every time I laid down for a few minutes. There was at least one arrest a week during the four weeks I stayed there, but for all its faults, it was kind of nice.

It was nice because I was in the heart of the city, what Greg called the northern Atlanta, and that was exactly where I wanted to be. Every time Jordan talked about his dream vacations to Savannah and Washington D.C., the best I could come up with was that I would like to see New York at some point, but not the tourist areas, the city itself. Thinking about these childhood conversations, I rode the subways all over the place, and even got some decent writing done in the process. I chatted with the little Asian woman who sold me two oranges every morning from the market below the SRO and got used to picking up coffee in blue cups from a cart on the way to subway. I walked everywhere I could think to go, and especially hit what I considered to be the important landmarks like Stonewall and the Apollo. I intentionally, as if reliving childhood talks with Jordan, avoided the major tourist attractions until a later trip to the city. As such, I spent my time watching and listening to the people and visiting neighborhoods and places I read about in books over the years.

By the time the first of August rolled around, I was ready to go home. I called Lena, and she told me Claire was looking for me. I had not talked to Claire in a few months, so I spent some cash at a pay phone in Edison, New Jersey to see what she was up to. Her and Devin were thinking about relocating to Atlanta, and she said she also had some big news. Although it wasn't the fastest route, I was planning to go through Savannah because that was a place Jordan always wanted us to go. I told Claire this, and she suggested we meet in Augusta after I visited Savannah. I agreed to call her when I was done in Savannah and headed south for the next fifteen hours – with only three stops along the way during that time. I landed in Savannah, and checked into an economy motel called the Master's Inn in Garden City.

It took me a week to visit all the places Jordan wanted to see in Savannah. I cried at six different ones, and each time, it felt like a good thing. I wrote Jordan – or his ghost maybe – detailed letters about each spot the same way I did with the places in New York, D.C., and Charleston, and I made myself imagine what it would have been like to go to those places together. I wondered if he would have joined the kids break-dancing by the river in the afternoon. I thought about how his eyes would have lit up at the historic churches. I walked the beaches on Tybee Island imagining the feeling of his hand in mine. After I experienced everything he outlined as his dream vacation, I called Claire and made my way to Augusta.

CHAPTER 6

"What was up with that guy outside," Claire asks as we take the same seats we spent so much time in when we were teenagers. The bookstore hadn't changed much, and they still had the same coffees, pastries, and wooden chairs that kept the younger versions of ourselves company as we finished our time in high school. She was asking about this guy named Brandon I was talking to outside the place – in the same spot Jordan and I once had one of our most intense conversations – when she arrived.

"He's trying to make some difficult love decisions, but he's scared of getting hurt," I say smiling at the similarity of this moment to the many bygone times we sat in these chairs talking about random tidbits of our lives. Claire has changed her appearance a lot since I last saw her, and during this conversation, I will learn that this is more important than I thought when I noticed. Whereas she always dressed somewhere between what folks might call masculine and feminine – with an especially deep interest in band t-shirts and dark colors – her appearance tonight would probably lead most people to assign her as male or a guy on sight.

"Ha," she says in a loud voice, "I guess he picked the right person to talk to."

Smiling, I say, "I actually kind of surprised myself."

"How so?"

"He was trying to figure out if he should take a chance that would allow him to continue falling in love with great people even if that meant he might end up getting hurt worse than he could imagine, and, shit, I don't know, I didn't even think about it before I just said hell yeah, you should do it, I would, no question at all."

"Wow, really?"

"Yeah," I say and take a sip of my coffee. "And the funny thing, especially in light of my history, I mean, is that, well, I mean it. I would do it all over again knowing the outcome, is that crazy?"

"I don't think so," she says stirring her coffee. "I mean, weren't some of the best moments of your life with Jordan? I mean, I don't

© KONINKLIJKE BRILL NV, LEIDEN, 2019 | DOI 10.1163/9789004392212_006

think I would give up my time with Devin no matter how it ends up down the road, so, I would say it just sounds like you feel like the pain was worth it or something like that." I spend days thinking about that explanation, and in the end, I think it's still the best way I could describe it.

"That's basically what I told him," I said, "But I don't think I even knew I felt that way until talking to him tonight." We both laugh at this, and silence descends for a few seconds while we each take sips of our drinks. "So," I say, "Enough about me, you said you were planning to move to Atlanta, and wanted some advice?"

"I was just wondering if you have any connections to medical people in the area because we might need that if we do relocate," she says, and I notice her voice is much softer, more hesitant, than usual. "It's okay if you don't, and we don't even know if we're moving yet, it depends on my work and Devin's work, you know, but I just figured I would ask because the other stuff, you know housing and all that, we've got a good handle on, but medical stuff might be tricky at this point in our lives." She is dipping her head and looking around us as if her words might be dangerous. It reminds me of the night we first met when we were talking about danger at parties in a parking lot, or when she first asked me about setting up Charlotte with Abs in high school. Something is going on, and I decide to just ask.

"Hey," I say, and she looks back at me. I meet her eyes, and ask, "Is something going on because you seem much more nervous than I've seen you in a long time?"

Running her hands through the buzz cut that looks quite fitting on her, she says, "Well, that's kind of the news I wanted to talk to you about."

"I'm game."

"Well," she says speaking slowly, "Do you remember Sam, you met him once during your quiet period, do you remember him?" I barely remembered meeting someone named Sam while passing through Columbia on my way to visit Abs up in Rock Hill a few years back, but I didn't remember much. He was cute and funny. He was Claire's best friend in college the whole time they were in school at USC. That was all I remembered.

"Not really, or, I remember him, but not much about him other than he was cute."

"So, uh, you don't remember that him and I were going to those meetings throughout college together?"

As if buried somewhere in the recesses of my brain, a memory popped back into focus. We were standing on the porch of the bungalow Claire and Devin shared, and she wanted me to look over some documentation for these support groups. I got angry at first because I thought it was another damn grief counseling thing like the one Abs tried to get me to go to, but it wasn't anything like that. Instead, it was this checklist and support program for people seeking gender confirmation – though it used different words – procedures and options. She had a friend that was transitioning and wanted her to accompany him to the meetings just in case they were not as positive as they appeared on paper. She wanted my opinion of the materials and had also reached out to Nick down in Florida for advice about it as well. "You mean the gender confirmation group, is that what you're talking about?"

Visibly relaxing, she says, "Yeah, that one."

"And Sam was the friend?"

"Kind of," she says, and then takes a deep breath. "Sam and I were both the friends."

"Really," I say smiling at her and reaching out to take her – maybe his now I thought in the moment, maybe it had always been his I thought – hand.

"Yeah."

"So," I said, "Have I been misgendering you for years now, and owe you a really big apology?"

"No, not really," they say smiling at me, and starting to sound more like themselves. Good, I thought, that seemed to relax them a little bit. I knew from too much experience this was not an easy moment for them. I waited as they remained quiet for a few moments. After taking a sip of their coffee, they said, "For Sam, it was that way, you know, he has always been a man, and always knew it. He says his body never really fit, like at all, that he can remember, but for me, it's been more of a gradual recognition kind of thing, more like how you thought you were a woman and wanted to transition, but realized you were kind of both a woman and a man in one body, kind of like that, but for me it's been more of a lifelong pull to realizing I am a man and probably always was, you know, or would have lived as one – whatever body I had – if that option had been more easily available to me, I don't know, does that make any sense?"

"Well, I would say that makes perfect sense, and I've already met many people who experience what Sam did, what you have, and what I have so I would say it's just different paths depending on the ways each person is, I mean, this is your path." They smile, and I add, "But I do apologize if I should have been more aware or helpful and failed to do so."

"I don't think you did," they say smiling, "I mean, I think reconnecting with Jordan and meeting you actually helped a lot, the same way being with Devin, hanging out with Charlotte, and meeting Sam helped me a lot. I mean, you know, I always got to be more boyish with my dads and with my mom, and with Devin and with y'all, but I caught so much hell for it as a kid everywhere else, and I don't know, I think I needed that freedom to find myself again as I got older." A small smile creeps across their face, and I return one of my own.

"So, do you need to know about the medical stuff because you may seek confirmation surgeries or hormones, because if that is the case, yes, I do know some people and Lena's partner, Lucy, works in the medical field – alongside the art she does, if you didn't know that yet – and knows a lot of good people too."

"Yeah, but more so, I need to be ready for follow up now because I've already scheduled and planned my top surgery later this year, and one of the people Devin works with is helping me do a legal name change right now, so it's more that I want to be prepared if I do need hormones or want bottom surgery later, does that make sense? I mean, I just have such great support in Columbia, and that is the main reason I'm hesitant about moving, but at the same time, Devin and I both may have great work opportunities coming in Atlanta so I want to be ready for that so we can make the best decisions. He says we'll do what we need to because he doesn't think any work thing is worth putting me in a bad spot otherwise, but I don't want to "have" to stay somewhere if it turns out we'd be better off somewhere else in other ways."

"Makes perfect sense to me, and if you come to Atlanta, we'll get you set up," I say smiling and rubbing their hand. "Do you have a pronoun preference, like me with they, and do you want us to start using your chosen name now or what would be best for you?"

Laughing more freely than any time in the conversation thus far, they say, "And that kind of question is why I wanted to meet up with you first out of the bunch."

"You always accepted me, I'm just returning the favor love."

"I go by Clark now, and it will be legal by the end of the year according to Devin's co-worker, and I do prefer to be called he, which was tricky at my work at first, but they're catching up faster than I expected honestly."

"It is a pleasure to meet you Clark," I say smiling, and he laughs and motions for me to come over to his side of the table. We share a hug in the middle of the café area, and I volunteer to update our Atlanta family on the changes taking place, and to start getting medical resources together in case him and Devin come to live in our city. That night, we stay with Charlotte at the house her and her partner share in south Augusta, and her partner, Lori, introduces us to this amazing documentary series she found exploring the lives, history, and politics of lesbian women in America. We sit up most of the night watching the films, laughing about old times and recent events, and having more than our fair share of cigarettes, wine, and smiles.

CHAPTER 7

"Fuckin' dykes," the passenger in an old blue Ford pickup truck yelled as Lucy and I walked together in Buckhead heading in the direction of Fantasyland Records so she could pick up a new CD from Tracy Chapman released earlier in September. I also had my eyes on a couple new releases that September, but my reasons for going with Lucy were more complex. I had been wrestling with some questions since I was out on the road, and I thought she might be my best source of information especially since I wasn't ready to talk to Lena or Abs about it yet.

Laughing, because we were kind of used to this stuff by our mid-twenties, Lucy said, "I guess you're a lesbian today Kid." It wasn't my first day being assigned to this category, but as usual, it felt odd that simply wearing a nice skirt and walking down the road with a woman could change my gender and sexuality in the eyes of other people. It always made me wonder just how fragile such concepts were if they could so easily be mistaken in the midst of guessing games.

Matching her laughter, I said, "Well, I guess I managed to appear female today, there's that." As I did when I was much younger, I felt proud every time I both felt more feminine on a given day and was read as such by others even though I would have – echoing the reactions of most, for lack of a better phrase full time, trans and cis women I knew – happily done without the slurs and fear that went along with being read as a woman.

"Well, I did have a thing for butches when I was younger," she said skipping over a puddle as we turned onto Pharr Road. I blushed, clutched my chest, and did a bit of curtsy that led Lucy to slap the side of her leg laughing at me.

"Speaking of butches, Lori, you know Charlotte's partner I told you about," she nods, "Said there used to be a lot more butches around, is that true?" A proud Butch herself, Lori outlined this theory in impressive detail, and seemed – I would say understandably – sad about it.

© KONINKLIJKE BRILL NV, LEIDEN, 2019 | DOI 10.1163/9789004392212_007

"I don't know," Lucy says laughing, "But it feels that way to me too."

"I wonder what happened," I say lighting a smoke, and remembering all the historical stuff Lori shared with Clark and I while we stayed with her and Charlotte. It reminded me of other things that seemed to change while I was growing up. I remember being considered a cross dresser in the 90's, but these days, almost no one used that term, and instead I was non-binary or genderqueer or gender fluid. I didn't know, I still don't, which term I liked better, but it was interesting the ways languages, patterns, and identities seemed to shift over time. Lena had also noticed that a lot of – mostly economically privileged and white – people were using the term pansexual these days – sometimes with the same definitions we always used for bi and queer when we were younger and other times while trying to redefine bi and queer in new, more limited ways. I felt the same way about the new terminology for sexual fluidity. I didn't really know what term I preferred, but it seemed to me that the terms didn't matter as much as trying to get rights and the ways we treated each other and were treated by others. I didn't know it at the time, but the coming years would include a lot of discussion on terminology that always made me wonder if we were being distracted from our shared problems by arguing over what we called ourselves and other people like us. I didn't know the answer then, and I still don't.

"No clue," Lucy says as we arrive at Fantasyland, "But for now, I just want to get this album for Lena so I can hear her do that giggle uncontrollably and bounce all around the house over new music thing she does." She does an impression of the way Lena freaks out over every new album, and we both start laughing again as we enter the record store.

"It is one of the most fun things ever, I have to admit."

"I know, right?"

For the next half hour, we roam around the shop looking at records in different formats. I pick up a copy of the Rolling Stones' new album, and she picks up a copy of the Tracy Chapman album for Lena and a copy of the new Against Me album for herself. The shop, best I can describe it, was simply a large, cluttered room full of music.

It was the type of place that Lena or Abs could spend a whole day in without even noticing. The two of them, independently or together, would get lost in stacks of records, tapes, and CDs as if they had found a magical world the rest of us could not see. For all my own love of music, I never understood the way it transported the two of them into some other space or place beyond the everyday world. I never understood it, but I loved witnessing it just the same.

As we left the store, Lucy said, "So, you wanted to come up here with me today, did you have anything specific in mind," and looked at me like she somehow knew she guessed right.

"I did," I said, "And, I mean, I do, but I know it's been a rough few days for you so I don't want to be a pain." Lucy had been struggling this week with her symptoms more than on the, as she put it, "average day." Part of her condition involved concrete-like mucus getting lodged in parts of her body that could make it hard to breathe, hard to digest foods, and hard to stay too far away from a restroom for very long. Lena and I had been looking after her this week because she experienced what she said was the worst flair up she had to deal with in a few years. At one point, she even called her doctors about the possibility of an oxygen tank, which was something that many people with CF had to use, but so far, she did not. I didn't want to ask for her help at a time where she was already dealing with a lot because I thought maybe that would be rude or insensitive or something like that.

As was often the case, I realized I should have just asked her instead of making assumptions when she laughed and said, "Are you kidding? Kid, this is my life, and whatever issues you're having that are not life and death are probably a good distraction."

"Are you sure, I mean, you already have to manage so much shit."

She about bends down on one knee on the sidewalk laughing, and I realize that shit is often the operative word. "Did you do that on purpose," she asks.

"Nope," I say kind of wishing I had.

"Would have been even funnier if you did." Regaining her composure, she says, "I get where you're coming from and I appreciate it, but I can tell when I'm trying to do too much, and so I'll let you know,

43

okay?" It made a lot of sense so I nodded, and she said, "The thing is, this is part of who I am, you know, and so I would rather you just act like normal, even on a tough week, and I'll be sure to let you know if you become a pain."

"I can do that."

"Good." She laughs and mouths the word shit again, "So, what's eating you?"

"It's kind of embarrassing."

"Ooh, this could be fun," she says smiling as we turn off Pharr Road heading back the way we came to the record store. "If it's about your friend Clark, Lena already filled me in, and I already got in touch with one of my friends who works with a supportive doctor so that is taken care of and you don't have to worry about it anymore."

"Thank you for that," I say noticing the shaking in my voice. I never have gotten used to how much harder or easier our lives can be depending on the connections we have. "But that's not it this time. It's something, well, more personal, but hard to say."

"Is this why you wanted me instead of Abs or Lena?"

"I don't know," I say, "I just don't know how to talk about this with them yet, but I know I will at some point. I mean, I don't know, I just think you might be better for this first."

"Okay," she says, "You've got my attention."

"I think, well, I don't even know if I can, but I think, damn, uh, I want to go to college, okay, that's it, can I, I mean, is that possible?"

"Oh Kid, of course it's possible."

"But I dropped out, you know, I quit after Jordan died, and I got the good enough diploma, I mean, but does that even count to colleges, I mean, can I take the SAT with that?" I stopped in the middle of the sidewalk, and kind of bowed my head. I was more than a little ashamed that while Abs, Lena, Greg, Charlotte, and Clark all got degrees, I didn't even have a high school diploma. Where we were from, it wasn't unusual for people not to finish or go beyond high school, but I felt like I should have been able to do it if all my friends could.

At the same time, I never did put too much emphasis on education before thinking about it while driving around the country. Hell, I only got the GED thing because Greg made me take the test. I was the most well-read person any of my friends knew, even compared to Abs they all said this repeatedly over the years, but in terms of credentials, I was unqualified for anything beyond menial labor. I felt like I gave up school as a kind of self-inflicted punishment after the accident, but it bothered me more and more since I started trying to enjoy my life again. I spent my entire trip over the summer thinking about it, but I didn't even know if it was possible to go to college without a diploma, in my mid-twenties, or without any real money.

"Well," Lucy says taking my hand, and raising my chin the way Lena often did when I was avoiding eye contact, "How did you do in high school?"

"Not great," I said thinking about all the days I skipped school so I could read the books I wanted to read and avoid the assholes in the hallways. Schools always felt about as uncomfortable as churches to me, and as a result, I avoided them more than I probably should have and only ever did the bare minimum I needed to in order to go to the next grade.

"Well, then I don't think you should take the SAT at all."

"Why not?"

"Because that is only necessary if you want to apply as a traditional student, and that might be harder for you if you didn't do well in high school, didn't finish high school, and don't want to go to like a tech school or something like that first."

"So, it's not possible, I thought you just said it was." I felt my chest deflate, and realized I wanted this more than even I had known before I said it out loud to someone.

"No, that's not what I'm saying," she said and gave me a hug. Maybe she could tell I needed one. In any case, it felt like one of the best hugs of my life. "I'm saying that you don't want to apply as a traditional student so you won't need the SAT."

"So then what kind of student would I be?"

"Georgia has a program for non-traditional students, and I bet you're eligible. What year were you supposed to graduate, or what year did you stop going?"

"Same year, 1999, why?"

"For the program, you have to have been done with high school for five years, and have either a high school diploma or, as you put it, a good enough diploma." She chuckles, "I'm guessing you could get into the program, and then you could go to GSU downtown, you just wouldn't be able to go to any private school, or get any scholarships at first."

"Well," I thought feeling myself become hopeful again, "How would I get into one of those programs?"

"I can get the information for you. You take a placement test instead of the SAT or ACT, and then you might have to take some remedial classes at the college before you're fully admitted, but that is about it. If you want to do it, I'll pick up the information after work one day this week."

"Um, Lucy, what's an ACT?"

"Don't worry about it, it's another college test that people take."

"And what are remedial classes?"

"If you don't score high enough, like on math or something, in the placement test, then they have you take a class in it to get you ready for college classes in the subject."

"I can do that," I say thinking I am almost certainly going to need to do so related to math as most of my knowledge of the subject is related to practical things – like paying bills – rather than abstract equations and such I remember from classrooms. "But, uh, Lucy," she nods and I continue, "How would I pay for this, any ideas?"

"I would guess loans would be your best option since you won't be able to pay for it with the jobs you have, you won't likely get any scholarships at first, and there aren't really any grants you would be eligible for that I can think of right now.

"Loans, like from a bank?" I cannot imagine a bank giving me a loan as I don't even have any credit cards or possessions of value. I don't even know for sure what credit is.

"No, not from a bank, but it works the same way. You can get government loans to pay for school, but you might be paying them back forever."

"I can do that," I say, "Kind of like how people who want to own houses take out a mortgage that they pay forever or for a long time?"

"Yeah," she says, "It would be kind of like that." We start walking again, and after a few minutes, we turn on Peachtree Road so we can make our way back to the train station. "What do you think?"

"I think I want to do it," I say, and then, though for some reason this question is even more embarrassing to ask than all the others, "But, I don't know, do you think I could handle college?" I don't know why, but I felt like I would get a better, or maybe more honest and less hopeful, answer from her than I might get from Lena or Abs or Clark or even Greg. I honestly thought the college thing was a pipe dream, but I also wanted to be wrong about that.

"I don't think you would have any trouble with college," she said, and I stopped in the middle of the sidewalk. I just stared at her, wondering if she was just being nice even though I knew that wasn't really her style and that she was one of the most blunt-honest people I had ever met. She looked back at me, and said, "It's okay if you don't agree, but that's my opinion." She didn't wait for me to respond. She didn't say anything else. She just turned back and continued walking toward the train station. Shaking my head, I remembered Lena telling me about many times where Lucy did the exact same thing after offering an opinion she thought did not deserve or warrant any kind of argument. It was her way of, as Lena put it, "driving home a point." It took me a few moments, but then I nodded. I nodded again and started walking too. I didn't agree with her, not yet at least, but I wanted her to be right. With this thought carrying my feet, I caught up with her right before we reached the station.

CHAPTER 8

I started attending college in January of 2006. With Lucy's help, I did all the paperwork and took the placement test the previous October – a couple weeks after our trip to the record store – and was told I could start the next semester. My first semester included one real college class, as I thought of it, and one remedial math class. I was surprised to see that I wasn't the oldest person in the remedial class, but I still felt like I was completely out of place on campus for a very long time. I traded in my job at the theatre for a night shift at the hotel near mine and Lena's apartment where I could do homework and reading during the early morning hours where almost nobody was awake, much less in need of hotel service.

My week became a routine where I would work four nights in row – Sunday through Thursday – and leave each morning for classes at Georgia State University downtown. I would take the train to the campus, go to my classes, and then take the train back to College Park where I could finally go to sleep. Sometimes I wandered through the same hallway where Lena and I went to an event on poly relationships when I was still a visiting high school kid and remembered how I planned to come to this school with Jordan right after graduation. "Better late than never," I often thought as I left the hallway for the class I had nearby. Somehow, this activity became a ritual I continued doing throughout the first semester.

I liked being on the campus the same way I liked being on the campus down in Florida with Abs. There was something about the sound of people talking about ideas, about books, and even about partying that spoke to me on some level. I liked the freedom I felt roaming from one building to the other. It wasn't like where Abs was at because Georgia State was situated in the middle of downtown Atlanta, but it was still calming to see the banners and imagine that I really did belong in the classrooms for a while. In my mind, I was only going to be there for a short time before I had to get back to reality, but I had already decided to enjoy however long I remained a college student.

© KONINKLIJKE BRILL NV, LEIDEN, 2019 | DOI 10.1163/9789004392212_008

I figured that at the very least I might gain a few experiences to write about and maybe a few new writing skills along the way.

My friends were, in my opinion, a little too excited when I started school. I say too excited because I started school completely certain that I would fail out in a matter of time, and I worried they would be disappointed if they expected more than that. I saw it as a temporary diversion in my life, but they saw it as the real deal. I didn't know what to make of that. I also say too excited because they had more fun with my first few days of college than I did.

That may sound strange, but it was true. Lena got me a little blue lunchbox – the plastic kind we had when were kids – with a scene from a cartoon we used to watch on the floor at her parents' house. Abs sent me a care package filled with coloring books, crayons, a book of lullabies that were supposedly best for nap time, and a sippy cup in the school colors of Georgia State. Greg sat me down and began to explain the origins of the birds and the bees and the importance of understanding that my hormones should not lead me astray when I was supposed to focus on my studies. Even Lucy got into the act by waiting outside of my first class when it ended to do a surprisingly hilarious impersonation of a parent picking up their child from the first day of pre-school – she even brought me a snack.

As much as I hate to admit it, I enjoyed all these shenanigans because, somehow, they made me feel much less nervous about the start of school. I wasn't too concerned about the math class because I figured I could find my way through the requisite memorization and equations I would never need after I finished school the same way I did in high school. I was correct. I was, however, worried beyond words about my first real class – an introduction to American Literature. Writing was the only thing I ever felt like I was good at, and I was fairly certain that if I stood any chance in college, as my placement exam seemed to support, it was in the realms of literature, arts, and language. I took the class both because I thought it would be fun, and because I figured it would tell me if I had any chance in college beyond that first semester.

In the end, I had nothing to worry about. The class only covered things I had already read on my own, and in the end, the only thing I learned about the stories was that I had been mispronouncing many of the words, names, and places in them. I had never heard any of them spoken aloud, I realized in the middle of the class, so I figured this wasn't that big of a deal. About myself, though, that's where the real learning started. I realized that I loved talking about these stories with other people, and I especially loved it when other people interpreted them in ways that did not cross my mind. I would spend hours, especially on Fridays since I didn't have to work that night, sitting outside with other students – almost all of them were much younger than me, but I got used to that over time – talking about the stories.

During Spring Break, laughing that I once again had a Spring Break, I headed south to spend some time with Abs in Tallahassee. She was so excited that I was in school that we spent the week doing things she said every student should do. Halfway through my visit, we went to a poetry reading at this warehouse-type place, and I even got up during the open mic portion and read one of my sappy morose compositions for the hell of it. When I got back to my chair, she said, "I can't believe you did that," between short bursts of laughter.

"Neither can I," I said thinking I probably made a fool of myself, but happy to have done so hours away from where I lived. Lena, with her band and solo performances, was the one of our group most comfortable with the stage, and even Abs, especially now that she was in graduate school and working with students, was much better at such things than I was. My own approach had always been to find ways to hide in the crowd, make up stories about the people around me, and hope I didn't have to talk to anyone – much less a crowd – all that much. It was completely out of character for me to take the stage, and yet, it was kind of fun.

"You wanna get out of here, don't you," she asked smiling at me.

"More than words can say," I said, and she motioned to the door. We grabbed our bags and headed in that direction faster than was probably called for. When we got outside, I lit a smoke, and said, "Where you want to go?"

"Coffee," she barked before grabbing my hand, and heading off in the direction of the hotel and stoplight not far from where we were standing. In the other direction, as I learned driving around earlier in the week, was the football stadium and the broader scope of the Florida State campus. "Come on," she said picking up the pace as we reached Railroad Avenue, and she turned us to the right. Smiling, I realized we had arrived at the same hippie-looking coffee shop we went to when I visited the summer before. This time, I caught the words All Saints on the sign to the side of the building right before we reached the front door.

We grabbed coffees and headed out on the back porch I didn't yet know the place had. We sat down on opposite sides of a bench facing each other, and she said, "This is where the magic happens, this is where I write." She was smiling as big as I had ever seen in all our years together, and I wished I had a way to freeze the moment, maybe like a photograph or something to keep forever, so I could remember that sight.

"I like it," I said looking around at the, except for one other person reading a book about Bruce Springsteen, empty back porch with the wooden fence blocking off the rest of the neighborhood and creating the impression of privacy. "Is it always this quiet," I asked reading some of the graffiti drawn on the brick walls that made up the back of the coffee shop. Much of it was impressive, and I wondered about the ways Lucy and Lena would take it apart, explain the contours and color selections, and build new artistic designs from ideas it gave them.

"Most of the time, and especially at night," she said lighting a smoke, "And it's just dirty enough to feel like my old back porch during high school."

"Wow," I said, "You lived back there for a while."

"Yep, I miss it sometimes."

"Do you ever go back?"

"Nope, not since mom and dad moved down to Charleston."

"Hey, I always said finding the perfect Palmetto Rose was a full-time job."

"Naturally," she says laughing, and at that moment, the other person on the porch puts their book down, closes it in a gentle motion, looks up for the first time, and smiles. They check their watch, put their things in a bag, and start to get up from their own bench. They seem to be surveying the room for some reason, and I'm almost sure they are counting something, but I can't figure out what they're counting. I wonder about it for a second before Abs asks, "Do you ever go back, or have you been back even once."

"Nope."

"Do you think you ever will?"

"Every time I drove past it on the Interstate, I thought about going by Jordan's grave, but I never did it," I say looking off over the top of the wooden fence. The sky is almost purple, and there are about five stars in my direct line of vision. Something about the sight captivates me for a moment, and then I say, "I been thinking about it lately, to tell you the truth, so, I don't know, I might at some point."

Before Abs can respond, the other person says, "Hey Abs," on their way out the back door on the side of the porch. It is the type of wooden swinging door that I associate with back yards, and it makes a screeching sound as it opens.

"Hey Carina," Abs says with a smile and the other person disappears.

"What was that?"

"That's Carina, they're kind of quiet, and only come up here from time to time because they live on the coast," Abs says smiling, "We talk sometimes when it's just the two of us back here. They have family going to FSU right now and living in the little art park down the road so sometimes they come up to visit, and when they do, they like to hang out here and read."

"They were cute."

"Yeah, they are," Abs says blushing, "But anyway, I think it might be good for you to go back there someday, even if only for a few minutes or so, I don't know, maybe it would give you closure or something like that." I can tell Abs has a little crush on the Carina person, but I decide to let it go since she doesn't seem to want to talk about it. Not for the first time, I chuckle to myself at the tendency for Abs and me to have similar tastes in others.

"That's what I've been wondering about," I say with a smile. We keep talking for a few more hours, and the following days we spend just catching up and, well, kind of being kids again. She takes me to the museums in the area, and we go to a folk music performance in the art park near the hippie-looking coffee shop. We don't see Carina again, but I do meet a lot of the people Abs lives with in the graduate program. At the end of the week, I head back up to Atlanta, and prepare to polish off my first semester as a college student.

CHAPTER 9

Before I could blink, my first semester of college was over, and to my utter amazement, I had two A's to show for it. I could take the required math courses for an actual bachelor's degree whenever I was ready, and I was registered for four more classes over the summer. The summer courses were intense – my required college algebra course combined with other core classes in biology (easy, but boring), political science (the professor was dreamy), and another literary class where I had already read the entire syllabus before the first class – and it almost feels like that summer disappeared like the turning of a page because all I did was work, go to school, study, and repeat the cycle again for the entire twelve weeks.

One morning following an inability to sleep, I was drinking a glass of wine and puffing on a cigarette on my porch celebrating four more A's, and beginning to feel like Lucy might have been right when Lena slid into the chair beside me, and for the third morning in a row, said, "So silly, what about a major?"

I figured I would finally try to answer the question since I was going to need to figure it out anyhow. "I'm still not sure what a major is," I said laughing and watching the brown skin of Lena's exposed left leg reflect the sun. She had just woken up and was leaning back in her favorite chair wearing her usual old beat up t-shirt – this one was one of mine – and shorts pajama combo. Lucy arrived on the porch, also wearing one of my shirts I noticed with a smile, and handed Lena a cup of coffee before sitting in the chair on the other side of me.

"A major is like your main area silly, that's it, it's what you want to focus on."

"I thought you were going to focus on literature," Lucy says waving a strand of hair out of her face and taking a sip of her coffee. "Were you up all night?"

Pointing my wine glass at her, I said, "Yeah, I'm just amazed that I'm kind of enjoying this college thing, I don't know, I guess it's easier and more fun than I expected." I took a puff of my own cigarette, and,

© KONINKLIJKE BRILL NV, LEIDEN, 2019 | DOI 10.1163/9789004392212_009

as Lena and I were both getting good at, directed my exhale away from Lucy. It was one of the adjustments, like not smoking inside anymore, that we made because the smoke could be very dangerous – like even more than usual – for Lucy. She smiled at me, and I said, "I don't know about literature, I mean, I've read everything in those classes already, and I'm not really learning anything about writing I don't already know."

"What about biology or chemistry, you like reading about that stuff, and have since we were little," Lena said giggling. Lucy was making faces at her, and as usual, her reaction was kind of adorable for all of us. "I mean, I did communications, and went into music so it doesn't have to be exactly what you want to do later, I mean, it can be something you enjoy."

"Yeah," Lucy says making more faces at Lena in between statements, "My degree is in political science, and now I work in health evaluation and do my art, kind of related skills, but not an exact match or what I planned at the time."

"I don't think I would like biology though," I say finishing my glass. "It's very Baptist, and I'm not sure I could handle doing that much pretending for the rest of school."

"Baptist," Lucy asks.

"Yeah, it's all based on the belief that there are only two sexes, and everything is very hetero and mono even with animals, but that's not nature, that's a system we made up like 100 years ago or something, I read about it in a book by another biologist a couple years ago, and I don't want to have to pretend that real things, you know, like intersex or fluidity or stuff like that, don't exist just so I can pass some white guy's multiple choice test – doing that for the two required," and I put up air quotes with my hands, "supposed to be "sciences" was enough pretending for me."

Laughing and almost spilling her coffee, Lucy says, "I know what you mean, but you'll probably have to pretend a lot of stuff to get through college."

"I guess I thought college would be more about the real world, especially science, but like my political science class, I mean, I liked it but there were no trans people in those surveys and how am I supposed to believe that because 2,000 people said it to a researcher once in some General Social Survey that makes it a fact that can apply to the rest of the people."

Adopting what I can only call the most pretentious voice I can imagine, Lena says, "Well, the thing is, you have to have faith in the method."

"Yeah, I've done so well with faith in my life so far," I say and all three of us laugh as Lena continues talking about faith in that same tone for a few more minutes. I was only starting to realize that the big difference between science and religion, best I could tell, is which group of overly privileged, mostly white, mostly cis het men you put your faith in, and that neither group seemed to be all that familiar with the existence of bi or trans or other "sinful" or "deviant" (depending on which one's books you were reading) types of folk. At least with the scientific stuff, as Lucy pointed out and did in her work, we might be able to adjust the belief system more easily if more of us got into their ivory towers and revised their assumptions. I liked this idea and thought of the work Abs was doing down in Florida. Maybe I would ask her what major I should choose or maybe I would just pick one at random that seemed interesting.

I was still thinking about these things, and still uncertain what major I would choose, when I met up with Greg at a bar in East Point a few days later. Ever since the first night I went out in public dressed the way I wanted to dress as a teenager, I had a special place in my heart for East Point. It was not much like it had been then, but it was still a fun place to go all these years later. There was something about the families of varied races playing at the big park near the train stop, and the way all the parking lots filled up with people laughing on holidays that had firework shows that made me smile. I was meeting Greg at a bar he liked right by the train station and hidden above the row of shops on the street. I walked up the narrow staircase and entered the bar as its customary collection of smells – smoke, sweat, and various types of alcohol – hit my nose.

Greg was sitting on the left side of the bar in a booth with a handsome man about our age that I knew from the briefing Greg gave me for the night was his new love interest Sullivan. They looked cute together, and I stood there for a second watching them share a laugh.

I always liked to watch people when they didn't know someone was looking. There was something about those observations that seemed to reveal more about the people than I might get once they were aware of my presence and reacting to the potential interpretations of another. A few months later in another college class, I would learn that there were researchers who did this type of thing for a living while seeking to understand the taken-for-granted rules of a given group or culture. I liked that class a lot. I watched them continue to interact for a few more minutes.

"Glad you could make it," Greg says – likely aware that I was a few minutes late – as I reach the table, and slide into the seat beside him. "Kid, this is Sullivan, and Sullivan this is Kid." We said hello, and I ordered a beer from the attentive server who showed up within two seconds after I sat down. Sullivan had this calm demeanor that set me at ease almost immediately, and I wondered how useful that might be for a pastor. I was surprised, maybe my own assumptions about pastors at play, he was smoking, but I was too caught up in what I thought was a kind of haunted look in his eyes – somewhere between happy and sad like Clark often said about me – that felt all too familiar. After my drink arrived and following the usual get to know each other chit chat, another man arrived at the table looking sheepish – in truth, he looked terrified – and sat down beside Sullivan. "This is David," Greg said when I looked to him with, I'm sure, curiosity written all over my face.

"Sorry I'm late," he said in a voice that was more hesitant than anything else, "I was on the phone with the camp for longer than I expected."

"The camp," I asked.

"Yeah," Sullivan said smiling, "I just took a job at church here in town, and David took one working for a camp over in Milledgeville so we're getting all the details ready so we can move and all that stuff now that school is over." David and Sullivan were apparently best friends throughout Bible College, and they were both in the city celebrating this weekend. David had grown up in his family's church in a small town on the opposite side of Augusta from where I grew up, and Sullivan was settling into a sweet gig at one of the big churches in downtown Atlanta after also coming from a small town in Georgia.

Greg was excited and nervous about this long-distance relationship becoming more of an everyday part of his life, which, I learned later, was why he finally decided that Lena and I had to meet Sullivan. Lena had dinner with the two of them the night before, and she liked Sullivan, but did not think this was going to be the "one" for Greg. I had not made up my mind on the relationship, but I agreed with her that it was a good one for Greg so far.

We spent the next hour celebrating their new careers and sharing stories. Since both were from small towns like I was, we spent some time talking about some of the weird shit that Greg avoided growing up in the city. He always loved this kind of stuff, and both Sullivan – from a place called Possibilities – and David – from a place called Queens – had plenty of it. It also got me thinking about all the small towns in Georgia with insane names like Needham, Climax, Between, Hopeulikit, Experiment, and my personal favorite, Relee, Georgia over in Coffee County. It was enough to always make me wonder if the towns themselves had just gotten together and come up with the names for their own amusement. We were laughing about the time Sullivan's high school shut down for a day because some cows that got loose from a nearby farm were congregating at – and thus blocking – the entrance to the building when David left to go, as he put it, "check in with the old lady."

As he disappeared into the narrow stairwell, Sullivan clarified, "He's been seeing some woman in Milledgeville all summer, and they check in most nights."

"You don't sound like you approve," I said smiling.

"I don't, honestly," Sullivan said shaking his head. "It would be different if he was like me or you, you know," he said pointing back and forth between the two of us, "But he plays on Greg's team, so to speak, so I worry about him."

"He's gay?"

"Yep."

"Closeted?"

"Deeply, and in a lot of pain as a result," Sullivan says sighing, "He talks about coming out, but he's terrified of his family, and working through a lot of issues related to his faith and some bad shit that happened when he was a teenager."

"I get it," I say as Greg takes Sullivan's hand across the table. It's obvious that Sullivan cares for the guy, but we all know there isn't really anything anyone can do for David. I like seeing Greg with his hand across the table and smiling at Sullivan in a way I've only seen him look at a few people so far. "So, nights like this are his only time to be himself?"

"Pretty much," Sullivan says, and I nod. Silence descends over the table. Greg and Sullivan continue holding hands, and I try to imagine what David must be going through. The server returns, and we ask for our check. I talk them into letting me cover it as a welcome to the group gesture for Sullivan, and we all laugh when they inform me that Lena did the same thing the night before. As the laughter dies down, Sullivan says, "I guess y'all take good care of Greg here," while chuckling and taking Greg's hand again as we walk across the bar toward the exit.

"Yeah, he matters a lot to us," I say watching Greg blush.

"Sometimes a little too much," Greg says laughing as we hit the stairwell.

"What do you mean," Sullivan asks laughing.

"He's talking about the pit bull," I say and Greg and I both start laughing a little harder as we exit the building and step out onto the sidewalk. David is still on the phone outside, but he waves to us so we keep moving toward the train tracks.

Sullivan looks confused until Greg says, "Yep, Lena can become a bit dangerous and scary if anyone is even a little bit mean to either of us."

"That sweet and funny woman from last night?"

Laughing, Greg says, "That's because you're good to me, you don't want to see the side of her that came out whenever a guy wasn't good to me."

"I think I like her even more now," Sullivan says laughing as the three of us cross the street and head for the train station.

"And that is why you've only met the sweet and funny Lena," I say as we pass through the turnstiles and say our goodbyes before heading in opposite directions on the train tracks.

CHAPTER 10

There is no warning. There is no preview or time for preparation. All the books say this, but I don't know if you really understand it until you experience it for yourself. It is like being hit with a hammer that you didn't even know was there, or maybe like being thrown from a car or something equally unpredictable that leaves you completely incapacitated. It doesn't even matter if you prepare for it. Hell, I was prepared for it. I had been waiting for it for about two years, ever since being with Jackson opened the flood gates of my emotional baggage. It didn't matter. None of the journaling I did prepared me for it. None of the thinking about how I would manage it when the time came mattered at all. Nothing anyone could say had any effect. When it came, it was like I was drowning and there was nothing I could do about it.

I don't know how well my description matches up with other people who experience a depressive swing or episode. Based on all the books I read before and after those three days in the middle of August 2006, it seems like I was almost a textbook case. I woke up feeling like my body was heavier than it usually was, and no matter how hard I tried, I couldn't shake this feeling of impending doom and catastrophe. I stayed in bed most of the day even though I had things to do – things I wanted to do before that day. I barely ate, and I broke the no smoking in the apartment rule many times over the next 72 hours. I wasn't, best I could tell, physically ill, and yet, my entire body hurt the whole time as if being attacked by some unseen predator. I barely spoke, I didn't write, I just stayed in bed repeatedly telling myself to get up and do something without being able to make that happen.

At different times, Lena, Lucy, and Greg spent time in the room with me, but I barely noticed them. They even had Sullivan – who it turned out had lost someone early in his life as well – come by and try to talk to me. It didn't do any good, but it was nice to know he had days like those too from time to time. That helped me, for few seconds, feel less alone, but that tiny bit of relief was temporary and easily forgotten. Lena wanted to take me to the doctor, but we didn't

© KONINKLIJKE BRILL NV, LEIDEN, 2019 | DOI 10.1163/9789004392212_010

have health insurance, and both Sullivan and Lucy explained that there wasn't likely anything a doctor could do. Physically, I was fine, and so they guessed that two years of working through things had led to a moment of exhaustion that I would come back from in a matter of days or weeks. They were right, but until we knew they were right a few days later, it was more than terrifying to feel stuck in place like that.

When, as Abs put it on the phone, "my brain stopped attacking me," I tried my best to find something that caused the bad days. I knew from the books that this was a useless exercise because depressive swings rarely had any discernable external cause, but I felt like I had to be sure. I didn't come up with much in the process. In fact, the best I could come up with was the fact that I was happy had caused me to temporarily fall apart. As strange as that sounded, it was the best explanation. My life was good. I was doing well at work and at school. I was talking to people, and even dating occasionally again. I was happier than I could have imagined only a couple years before, and I thought maybe that was the source of the episode. It had been so long since I spent any time not thinking about what would go wrong that maybe my mind didn't know how to do that yet and would have to adjust. I still don't know if this makes any sense, but over time, I got used to occasionally having these episodes.

I was on the phone with Abs a week after my episode, as everyone including me was calling it, and she said, "I think sometimes the fact that we are not calculators is difficult because we often try to pretend we are that ordered when things are going well."

"I don't know what you mean Abs." The more time she spent in graduate school, the more I was getting used to having to ask her to explain the thoughts running through her head. It was a lot of fun because I felt like I was starting to get a free education every time we talked. Even better, she was always happy to explain whatever concept or idea she was interested in at the time in three or four different ways because she said it was good practice for teaching.

"I mean, you know, that we don't live our lives based on statistics, but we often pretend we do to make ourselves feel better, feel more safe I guess, when we're lucky enough to do so. Take the stuff you're dealing with, for example, you lost a loved one in an accident, and that was terrible and devastating for all of us, right?" I say yes, and she continues, "But see, most people walk around pretending that won't happen to them so they won't have to think about what it feels like, but we live in America and in the south where accidents happen every day, you know, even gun accidents and suicide attempts happen every day, so it could happen to any of us at any time, you know."

"Okay, so what Abs?"

"Well, we're not statistics or calculators so we don't think about the possibility of it happening to us any day because that might cripple us or keep us from doing anything," she says and I can hear both her smile and the wheels turning in her brain on the other end, "But when it does happen, like it did in our lives, we lose the ability to pretend it won't happen to us, we lose that shield or that belief in safety that other people are able to have faith in if they haven't seen it themselves. We don't get to look at this set of numbers and say it doesn't happen all that much or look at this other set of numbers and say but it won't happen to me. We already know it can happen, and we already know that it doesn't matter how often it happens because one time is enough to influence a whole lot of things in our lives."

"So," I say slowly, "You're saying that part of what I'm getting used to is that I know things on an emotional level, frightening things, that I could have ignored before."

"Yeah," she says, "You know, that's kind of it, these are not abstract events that happen to other people for you, they're not just numbers as one of my professors puts it, you have to be ready for them at any time because you can't pretend it won't happen to you."

"I don't know Abs, that's sounds about as depressing as possible."

"Or liberating," she says with a laugh.

"Liberating?"

"Yeah, think about all the people, hell our families even, who wake up at some point in their lives not sure if they've used the time well, regretting something they could have done, what do you think about that?"

"Well," I say, "It used to just seem normal, but nowadays, I feel like it doesn't make any sense because I only have a certain amount of days, who knows how many, left on the planet."

"And that's what I mean, you know, most people I've met and in studies we read are worried about doing the wrong thing, and that limits what they might do, but we already know things can go to hell even if we don't do anything wrong, and in some ways, I don't know, but for me, that means I can do whatever I want because I can't control the outcome anyway."

"I'll have to think about that," I say chuckling, "I understand what you mean, but I don't know if I'm there yet on the liberation aspect of all this shit."

"Keep trying," she says, "And you'll get there."

I was thinking about what Abs said as I pulled into the town where I grew up for the first time in seven years. I had been thinking about visiting Jordan's grave for a long time, but after talking with Abs, I thought it might be one of those things that I shouldn't put off or worry about anymore. It was what I wanted to do, and so I should do it simple as that. Making the decision did feel kind of liberating I had to admit. It was also helpful to talk to Lucy about what Abs said. Lucy agreed completely and pointed out that many people with her condition died young, and that many others had to carry oxygen or other tools everywhere they went just to live. She pointed out that while that was limiting in many ways, one thing it gave her was an unshakable desire to get everything she could out of every day. We were sitting at the punk club we went to in East Atlanta waiting for Lena's band to take the stage, and she said, "I just don't want to miss anything, and I think that's what Abs was getting at."

"But isn't that, I don't know, kind of exhausting."

Laughing, she says, "Of course, and like you recently, I have days where it is a war with myself to do anything or even just get out of bed, but I also know that any day could be the last, and that means that anything that goes wrong today might not be all that important, but that anything I put off today might be."

"So, I mean, what do I do, just embrace it – anything could happen so I might as well live as much as can and do everything I want to do?"

"Pretty much, I mean, think about it, what's the alternative?"

"Living in fear, I guess, since the fantasy Abs calls believing we're safe and indestructible isn't an option."

"And you tried living in fear, how was that?"

"Good point," I say thinking about what I was starting to call the lost five years. "It just seems like a hard adjustment to make, I mean, I don't even know where to start."

"It is hard, and it takes practice, but for me, I just started going for it, I mean, for what I wanted, and not listening to doubts or worries or anything like that, living in the moment I guess."

And that is what I was trying to do as I pulled up to the cemetery that Monday evening. At that point, I'd probably written Jordan a few hundred letters in the past year, but there was something about standing in his final home that was different. I never was one to believe in all that much, but I still hoped that he was out there somewhere. Out of all the things I could be wrong about, I thought, that would be a nice one. I stood there staring at the stone in silence for over an hour. I didn't think I would ever come back to this place after that night, and so far, that has been an accurate guess. I couldn't even imagine the strength it might take to live in this area again, and after I did what I wanted to do, I knew there wouldn't be anything left for me there. Wiping away the latest tear forming on my face, I said, "I miss you."

I put my hand on the stone, took a deep breath, and said, "I'll always love you, and I'm going to take you with me everywhere I go Jordan." I heard wind rustling through the empty field of stone tablets and lost loved ones, "But I have to say goodbye because I'm still here, and I think I'm ready to start over." I stood there for another thirty minutes or so as if there would be a response, but in truth, I already knew what Jordan would have said. We talked about it so many years ago after Daniel, and both agreed that if anything ever happened, we wanted the other one to keep going, find happiness, and not let this world win. We promised each other to do that, and that night, I came to see him one last time to tell him I was going to keep my word.

CHAPTER 11

The fall of 2006 went by in a blur. I was thriving in college classes, and I even ended up finally picking a major. It was strange to feel almost like my old self again, but also like a completely new person at the same time. I would ride the trains writing in my journals, and watch the people moving all over the city in various directions. I roamed around record stores with Lena and Lucy and met Greg – sometimes with Sullivan too – for drinks or dinner at least once a week. In October, after they decided they were not going to move just yet, I visited Clark and Devin up in Columbia for a few days. I was, well, for lack of a better term, feeling like I had a normal life again, and enjoying it more than I expected.

I continued writing Jordan letters that I would put in different places after they were finished. I told him about the cute religious studies professor, Dr. Allen, that I kind of followed around for a little while as he told me about different faiths and their interpretations of sexualities. I told him about the two dates I had – with a guy named Brian from my work and a woman named Marcy from school – that, while nothing all that special, occurred without any real freak outs. I told him about my growing collection of new skirts, and the shops where I found them. I told him about Clark's transformation, and listening to a mix tape Devin made for him years ago when he asked about a jazz band Devin was in love with. I played the tape all the way home from Columbia, once again using the beat-up Chevy truck paid for with more sappy morose poems. I told him that I didn't feel the same emptiness when I drove through the area where we grew up on Interstate 20, but that I also no longer felt even the slightest urge to maybe stop and look around. I told him everything, like I used to, but just in a new way.

I turned my ritual of getting rid of the letters into a little game. I would leave them in odd places and try to imagine – and at times write stories about – the people that might find them. In my head, these people felt an uncontrollable urge to read them and try to figure out who we were. I left some of them in college classrooms, others in restaurant bathrooms, and still others in the pockets of new and used clothes in different stores I visited. I put some of them into the sleeves of vinyl and compact disc albums that were created by artists Jordan liked. I even left a couple on gas pumps in between Atlanta and Columbia during my trip. To this day, I still wonder if anyone ever read the letters, and if they did, what they might have thought. I guess I'll never know, but it is fun to imagine the possibilities.

I was thinking about this while listening to an album one of my classmates gave me a copy of when Lena came out on the porch the day after Thanksgiving. "Are you listening to that same damn song again silly," she said laughing and sitting with her legs crossed in her usual chair. She brought the remainder of the wine bottle I was drinking from, and a glass for herself. As she topped off mine and filled her own, she asked, "What is it about that song?"

"I don't know," I said laughing, and realizing that I had been playing the song on repeat for close to two hours while I was finishing a project for my Humanities class. "I think I like the fact that I have both agreed with this song more than words, and currently would scream the opposite with all my might, I don't know, it just kind of hits me." The song was by a band called the Drive-by Truckers that were out of Athens, Georgia, and completely new to me. The song, called "Goddamn, Lonely Love," was, for me, about a guy trying to kill a painful breakup or loss, and I remembered feeling that way for years even though now I wanted to hang onto the love without the constant sense of loneliness. The song just spoke to me and led me to start looking for records by the band every time I went to a music store. My classmate had been playing the record while we worked on a project together, and I just fell in love with the thing so he made what he called a "burned" copy – a new word to me at the time – and I'd been blaring it every day since. I was lucky that Lena liked the song because otherwise she may not have only picked on me about the repetitiveness.

"I guess that makes sense," she says tossing her hair and lighting a smoke. "How is the project going?" For my humanities seminar, I had to compose an original story that was based on my life, and I was struggling with it more than I would like to admit.

"I don't even know," I said laughing and taking a sip of my wine.

"Let me see," she said reaching out for my notebook. I handed her the pages I was working on – for the past two hours – and chuckled as the song started again.

"Can we at least hear the rest of the record for a little while," she asked scanning the pages and chewing on her lip. She took a puff off her cigarette as I switched the track to another song called "Danko/ Manuel." I wasn't sure what the song was about, but I liked it a lot too. "Damn silly," she said after a few minutes, "This is good, I mean, it's intense or something I don't know the word, but I mean, this isn't just for your class, is it?"

"I don't know what it's for," I said smiling, "Maybe it's more for me, but I'm using the class project to try it out, I don't know." The pages were about Jordan and me – how we met, what it was like when we were kids, and our secret meetings at the park near our respective homes. "I have to write about something based on my life, so I figured I would try to write about us."

"How does that feel?"

"Difficult to say the least," I say as she continues scanning the pages. I light my own cigarette and take a sip of my wine. I can't decide if I'm struggling with this assignment because I'm not good at this kind of writing, or because it's not an easy subject to write about. The professor in the class said that writing about our lives can be therapeutic, and I'm hoping that is the case with this attempt, but I don't know if I believe her.

"Oh Silly," Lena says laughing and pushing the papers aside for a second, "I still can't believe I missed it when you were looking through my closet." She takes another puff off her cigarette, and says, "That seems like so many lifetimes ago."

"Yes, it does."

"It's so strange reading about myself," she says giggling and turning to the next page.

"I can leave you out if you want."

"No, you cannot," she says waving her cigarette. "It wouldn't be your life without me," she adds and sticks her tongue out at me.

"That's true."

"You gotta do Abs next, I want to see that."

"She'll kill me."

"Isn't that worth it for my entertainment?"

"Maybe, but for real Lena, what do you think? Will it be good enough for class?"

"I think so," she says, "You might even do more with it."

"I don't know about that," I say laughing as the album continues to play, and she hands me the papers back. The assignment is twenty-five pages, and I now have about eighteen so I guess I'm doing okay. I can't tell if it's any good, but I hope it's good enough for a passing grade in the class. I decide to just take a break and hang out with Lena for a few hours. Her band is playing later that night, and I'm looking forward to it even more than usual because she's going to play two Lucinda Williams songs I love for the first time.

Two weeks later, the semester is wrapping up, and I'm on campus to finally turn in the story and declare my major. For the major, I came very close to following Abs into the land of History, but for some reason, History degrees at my school require more foreign language work than I think I would be good at, and I don't want to risk paying for classes I might not do well in that I don't need for a job that can ultimately pay for the classes. As a result, I started gravitating to the other social sciences since they allowed for computer and statistic work to replace foreign languages in the requirements. Throughout the semester, I paid a lot of attention in the psychology, political science, and sociology classes I took alongside my humanities seminar. While in some ways these fields were just as backwards as the physical sciences, they at least seemed to at least have heard of bi, trans, and other minority groups even if they almost never mentioned these groups explicitly in their textbooks.

As I walked by other students on my way to turn in my paper, I was still going back and forth between the three options. Political science was interesting, but there was a lot of focus on rationality and other things that you rarely saw among actual people. Psychology, while again interesting, felt very conservative – and kind of Baptist – because they tried to explain everything through the individual (the soul as Baptists called it) or biology (human nature as the

Baptists called it), and I wondered if that would annoy me because the explanations seemed so much like the Sunday School classes of my youth. I turned in my paper and started to leave the building when I noticed a flyer for a course on Sexualities. Curious, I stopped and learned that it was offered by the sociology department. Sociology seemed very ahistorical, a little abstract and disconnected from the world I grew up in, and almost obsessed with trusting statistics that did not require venturing into the actual social world, but the sexualities class sounded interesting. Figuring, as Lena said, I could always change it later, I picked sociology and headed to the office where I could make that official. I figured it seemed at least a little more based in reality than the other options, and I could always keep taking all the arts and humanities classes I wanted as electives.

Part of me still wanted to major in a more artistic field, but since I needed something more likely to have a job at the end of it than what the stuff I was reading online said about the humanities and since I still had not had a book assigned in any of those classes that I wasn't already familiar with, I decided to try to be what I thought was practical. The same way Lena majored in communications and did the music thing on the side just in case she never made a living as a musician, something she was doing for a living now, I decided to put practical goals – income, food, maybe even security – forefront, and do the art I wanted to on my own time. I turned in the form at the office that day, and part of me hated my decision while the rest of me thought it was the best option for me at the time. I still don't know which was correct, if either of them were. I was kind of in my own world – wrestling with options in my head – as I walked through the hallways, reached the exit, and stepped outside into the sunlight.

"Hey! Watch out, you prick," a woman with amazing auburn hair said as I almost knocked her to the ground before I even noticed she was there. Grabbing her bag off the ground, and glaring at me with eyes that I bet could have killed me, she said, "What the fuck is your problem, why don't you watch where you're going asshole?"

"I, uh, I," I started to say, but before I could get the apology out of my mouth, she shook her head and started walking away from the building – or maybe just away from me – with impressive speed.

I didn't know what to do. I was glued to the spot. On the one hand, I wanted to apologize because I had been an asshole not paying attention to where I was going, and I could have hurt her as a result. On the other hand, I didn't want to follow her down the road, and even accidentally become the latest example of street harassment or creepy-asshole-following-a-woman in her life. Damnit, I thought, the one day I dressed more like a dude, but then I wondered if that would even matter vis-à-vis the possibility of following her. I took a step forward. I stopped. Shit, I thought, what do I do?

I could just barely still see her a few seconds later when I decided not to follow her. I didn't want to make an already terrible moment any worse, and I could always just apologize if I saw her on campus again. Even after I made the decision, however, I kept watching her. She moved down Central Avenue, and I watched her auburn hair flowing behind her. After a few minutes, I shook my head, and turned towards the train station. I began walking toward the station, but I couldn't stop thinking about her, wondering who she was, and wondering if I would see her again. I didn't have any clue, at least not then, why I kept thinking about her, and it started to annoy me about halfway through my commute home.

CHAPTER 12

"Does it seem funny that she was wearing one of those Palmetto Rose shirts like the one Abs has," I ask as Lena, Lucy and I sit on the couch watching some show about rich kids in California that Lena has fallen in love with for some reason. It is the night before New Year's Eve 2006, and the night before Lena's big concert ringing in 2007. We are just relaxing on the couch together like we often do, but I have to get up in a minute to go meet Greg for drinks.

"What are they talking about," Lucy asks.

"Silly has a crush on a woman they almost killed on campus."

"I do not have a crush," I say sounding more defensive than I would have liked, "And I did not almost kill her, I just knocked her over by accident."

"Silly is also in denial about the crush they have on the woman in question."

"Shut up Lena," I say, but they both just laugh. I wonder, as I often do, if my friends and I will ever grow tired of picking on each other. I doubt it.

"Why would it be weird that she has a novelty t-shirt that Abs has," Lucy asks when the laughter dies down after lasting longer than I thought was warranted.

"Because it gives them a chance to talk about her again," Lena says and sticks her tongue out at me. I'm on break in between semesters, and even though I would not admit it to Lena or Greg, I am aware that I keep talking about this random woman I almost met on campus. I don't think I have a crush. I'm just curious about her for some reason, simple as that. It's no big deal, I keep telling Lena and Greg and myself, there was just something about her, and so I think about her – and write about her – a little bit, that's all.

"Awe, that's kind of sweet," Lucy says as she reaches over and messes up my hair.

"It's not like that," I say, "I'm just curious about her."

"Say what you want silly, but I know that look in your eye."

© KONINKLIJKE BRILL NV, LEIDEN, 2019 | DOI 10.1163/9789004392212_012

"I don't have any look in my eye."

"Yes, you do, it's the same one you had when you came back from soccer talking about some jerk that kissed you when you were little." I have no clue what look she is talking about, but there is something exhilarating and equally terrifying about her statement. I did remember coming home and whining about the jerk – Jordan – after we first met. It is hard to believe that was almost twenty years before this conversation took place.

"Woah, Lena, that's a hefty comparison," Lucy says and sits back to look at the two of us on the couch.

"I'm not saying it's the same thing, okay, I'm just saying I've only seen that look in their eyes once before, and I know what it meant last time."

"I think you've been watching too many teen dramas," I say, and Lucy almost falls off the couch laughing. I get up from the couch and start getting ready to meet up with Greg and Sullivan at the bar over in East Point. We're supposed to have drinks together before Sullivan heads out of town for the weekend to see some friends he grew up with down in South Georgia. I pick out a lavender skirt I found at a thrift shop in Greg's neighborhood, and put on my own Palmetto Rose shirt I picked up in Charleston while I was traveling just to give Lena a laugh on my way out the door.

A couple hugs and pecks later, I head for the train station, and find myself walking behind a young couple for a few blocks. The guy looks familiar, and I'm almost certain Lena, or maybe Greg, knows him. I want to say his name is Ethan or Edward or something like that, but I don't care enough to say anything or try all that hard to remember. He's walking with someone he calls Cat, and they're talking about graduating from college as I turn right for the train station and they continue walking straight, likely headed to one of the few eateries around here. As I cross the railroad track I notice that the hotel I work at is especially packed tonight, and I figure that means I'll be dealing with holiday visitors soon.

As I sit down on the train, my phone goes off and scares me in the process. Even after a couple years, I'm still getting used to having one of these things, and even more so to the idea that anybody can find me at any time. Of course, I can and often do ignore the thing and any calls, but it still seems strange to be in potential contact with others at every moment. I remember disappearing into the woods or somewhere else as a child, and the joy, well freedom, of knowing that nobody could find me if they wanted to, and that no one would have any clue where I was. It felt like that was gone with the introduction of these cell phone things – and even more so a couple months later when Lena showed me something called social media. At the very least, some phone company likely knows where I am most of the time, and I wonder if this shift will cause us to miss out on some of the freedom and anonymity I recall from youth. It's a question I will continue to ponder as cell phones – and then smart phones – become more and more common throughout the coming years, but I still don't know how I feel about it.

I look down at the tiny screen on the outside of the flip phone, and see that Abs is on the other line before wondering if "line" is still the operative word. I flip it open and say hello. "Happy all the holidays and none of them to you," Abs says chuckling. It is her standard "I don't celebrate holidays, but I like an excuse to party" greeting this time of the year. "I'm surprised you answered the phone, I've kind of gotten used to you missing the call and calling back in a few minutes when you figure out what to do with the thing."

"I'll get the hang of it one day," I say sharing her laugh, "Usually, I'm still surprised it's there when it goes off. What can I do for you doc?"

"Nothing, really," she says, "I'm spending the holiday in Apalachicola, this little bay area on the coast, and I just wanted to say hey cause I was staring out at the horizon, it's beautiful here, you know, and thought about all the times we sat on the river dreaming."

"That sounds cool."

"It is," she says, and I can hear the smile on her face through the phone. "I was also reading your story, and I wondered why I'm not in it."

"I thought you would kill me if I didn't capture you right."

"I would," she says laughing, "But I'm a good editor so you'll be fine."

"I got a good grade so I'm already fine now that it's done."

"I think you should keep writing it."

"Why?"

"It might be good for you, and you could make it a book about us like you always joked about when we were being goofy teenagers dreaming about the future."

"You mean you want to read it."

"Well, I was saving the important reason for the end, of course."

"I don't know about that," I say trying to imagine if I could even do that. It's an idea that I'll play with for years, but one that I remember feeling so intimidated by at the time.

"Think about it, okay?"

"I'll think about it," I say as I get off the train at East Point and start making my way to the bar. The night is quiet, and a little chillier than I would have preferred. For a moment, I catch a glimpse of autumn hair, and before I even realize it, I'm walking toward it at a faster pace. It's not her, I realize a second or two later, but it strikes me that I wanted it to be her. Maybe Lena is right, I think, and at the same time, I hope not. At that moment, I become aware of Abs saying hello a couple times, "Yeah, sorry, I'm here, I just got distracted."

"No worries," she says, "But, really, you should think about it."

"I will, I promise," I say unsure if I'm lying or not.

"Okay, well, have fun," she says, "I just wanted to say hey, and when my friends get back, we're headed over to Richards Island to see some friends and do some karaoke so this was about the only time I had to chat before the new year comes. I already told her but tell Lena to break a leg again for me." I tell her I will and to have fun too. After a few failed tries, I manage to turn the phone off. I walk up the narrow staircase and feel the heaviness of the air in the bar hit me as I reach the top. There are people playing pool and darts and in some cases, it almost seems like both at the same time on the right side of the place tonight. Greg and Sullivan are in the same booth we usually sit in on the left side of the room, and I make my way over to the booth. I start chuckling as I sit down, and they both ask me what is so funny. It takes me a second to catch my breath as I sit down.

"A Sullivan's Island shirt, really Sullivan?"

Sharing my laughter, and obviously enjoying the reaction, Greg says, "He thought it would be funny, I wasn't so sure."

"One of the parishioners gave it to me for the holiday," Sullivan says smiling. "Looks like I'm not the only one advertising Charleston tonight."

I look down at the shirt I forgot I was wearing, but before I can speak, Greg says, "Yeah, but that's a little different isn't it?"

"Shut up Greg."

"What," Sullivan says.

"Kid's got a crush on someone they met wearing a similar shirt, and those damn roses have been a running joke for them and Abs since they were children," Greg says laughing. A server arrives with their drinks and takes my order. I light a smoke and give one to Sullivan when he asks. He's in the process of quitting, as he puts it, "a little bit at a time." Looking across the table, I love how happy the two of them look, even if Greg is being annoying about the crush stuff, and I wonder how long they'll stay that way. They recently realized that they disagree on one major point – Greg desperately wants children no matter how hard it is to be a parent, a gay parent at that, in our country, but Sullivan wants nothing to do with children. I'm more than impressed, so is Lena, that they're handling it well. They're talking through options, sharing how they each feel about things, and seeing what it means for them going forward. When Greg first told us, Lena and I both worried things were about to go bad fast, but instead, they're working together and supporting each other as they figure it out. I'm rooting for each of them individually, but I also would love to see them work out as a couple. It's nice to see Greg with someone who truly cares for and looks after him the way he does for everyone else.

"Do you want to talk about her," Sullivan asks smiling and rubbing Greg's arm.

"Thanks mate, but there is nothing to talk about, I barely know her, and I'm not crushing on her, Greg and Lena are just having fun." I smile at Sullivan, and ask, "So, are you looking forward to your visit home?"

"I am, my two best friends still live there so it's always nice to see them."

"You going to try out the woods old fella," I ask Greg with a laugh.

"I think I might," Greg says, "But I want to talk to Lena first because her big showcase concert thing is tomorrow night, and we'd be gone before then. I don't want to let her down, but I think I do want to go see the woods after all." Lena is a little more nervous about the New Year's Eve show than any other in a long time. There are supposed to be agents and other professional types there, and I think she's worried about missing a big shot if she has an off night. The thing is, she never has an off night, but she won't believe that.

"Call her," I say, "But I can tell you exactly what she'll say, and you can too."

"She'll tell me to go be in love in the woods."

"The same thing you would tell her."

"Yep," he says, and we share a laugh. "I know, I just told her I would be at the show so I want to make sure she's cool before I go."

"I get that."

"What about you, you still have two more weeks before classes start again?"

"I'm doing as much nothing as I can, just relaxing," I say laughing, and Sullivan starts clapping softly in response. "It's been a busy couple of years with all the grief, starting school, starting to date again, and all that, I can use a break."

"That's good," Greg says, but then he adds, "After all, you probably need to warm up and get ready for your love affair with the woman you just met."

Sullivan smacks the table laughing, and I just give Greg a look that is supposed to translate into asshole. Together, they start planning my wedding, Sullivan even offers to officiate, and I start thinking I'm no better off than I would have been if I had stayed on Lena's couch being the butt of her and Lucy's jokes tonight. I'm blushing far more than I'm used to, but there is also something comforting about cutting up with friends about meeting someone new. Even though I'm sure I'm not really crushing on her, I'm glad they're having a lot of fun with the idea. About a half hour, I can't believe they had that much material, later, we move on to other topics, and spend the rest of the evening laughing the night away. The new year is right around the corner and laughing with friends seems a fun way to end this one.

CHAPTER 13

The next night, I was sitting on a ratty couch, I think it was once black, in the corner of a club on the east side of Atlanta watching bands ring in the new year. This was the fourth band of the night, and Lena's group was next and last. They had the coveted before, during, and after the midnight hour set, and were planning to do a countdown to the new year in the middle of their set where even the band stopped to kiss people at the appointed time. They were also planning to cover an Against Me song that Lucy loved for the first time, and Lena was excited to see how Lucy would react to this selection. I was sipping a draft beer, enjoying the couch I always hoped to claim every time I came here to see Lena play, and watching the mass of people spread out on the open floor and stage. Other than the bar stools in the other room, it was the only place one could sit and listen to the shows. The bar was dark, loud, smoky, and crammed with people near the stage, but I heard rumors that it wouldn't be smoky anymore for long.

Lena always said her music career began by accident, and this was mostly true. While she was studying communications and developing a fascination with poly relationships in college, she picked up a guitar and started playing on street corners, at the college, and occasionally at open mic nights in coffee shops. She called it her new hobby at the time, but she was very good even though she didn't yet like hearing that. It wasn't long before she was asked to sing for a band that played regular club shows in the area, and after realizing just how much she liked doing that, she started focusing her education on the ways she could use her communications studies to support a possible music career. She kept going with college, ultimately getting a bachelor's degree later, but started devoting much of her time to learning to play guitar better, taking piano lessons, and writing songs. She also started turning my happy-meets-morose poetry into songs, which I didn't like at first, though I changed my mind when I heard them. Before long, music occupied the center of her life.

© KONINKLIJKE BRILL NV, LEIDEN, 2019 | DOI 10.1163/9789004392212_013

She started playing a wide variety of gigs and promoting herself as both a solo musician and a component player for bands. I didn't know it at the time, but many of the people I met through her gigs were doing similar things while they tried to build careers. After college, she took what she still called "that day job" at a television station to make sure she had a backup plan, but she also played and sang for a cover band that did old Bob Dylan, James Brown, and Rolling Stones' songs at a bar & grill. She was also in another cover band that did country standards, and she co-hosted a karaoke night with the drummer from the country cover band. She only really sang duets and background vocals in the country band, but at karaoke she would light up the stage most nights in between the people who came to the bar to play around. She also was the lead guitarist for a punk band – though she rarely sung for this one at all – and did backing vocals for her friend – and back then, sometimes lover – Monica who headed a hip hop act that later moved on to work in New Orleans. Throughout all these engagements, she continued to play solo shows at small venues, open mic nights, and even opened for her other bands a few times.

The bands came and went over the years, but then she started her own group that played kind of a mixture of southern blues, Americana, and rock originals she, I, and sometimes we wrote. They also played a lot of covers from her time in other bands and her constant search for new albums she would love. Her band, as she was quick to say, even backed her for some of the gigs where she was listed as a solo performer. They released a couple of extended plays on cassette and compact disc and were starting to gain at least a bit of a local following. About a year before my afternoon with Jackson, Lena left "that day job" because she was making enough to live a meager life with music only. This was also the same time that she met and started, as she put it, "losing my damn mind over" an artist who did watercolors of various parts of the internal and external human body. This artist, Lucy, also worked a day job doing health evaluation, and luckily for all of us that were hearing about her, was just as crazy about Lena. The big difference was that Lucy loved her day job and considered her art simply to be a hobby or maybe a backup plan of its own. They started going to shows, writing songs together and with me later after my experience with Jackson, and spending time together arguing about the merits of this or that painter, musician or other artist. Almost three years later, I watched with a grin as Lena took the stage, Lucy waved to her from the crowd, and the show that would lead us into 2007 began with a cover of Bruce Springsteen's "The River."

Lucy was a surprise for me when I came out of my five-year fog. It wasn't a surprise that she was around – I noticed that much at least. It wasn't surprising that her and Lena were seeing each other and other people – that was Lena's preferred type of relationship. No, what was surprising was how much fun she was, and how well her and Lena connected over art, politics, and even their shared desire to date other people occasionally while having a primary relationship together. It was also surprising that Lena dated other people less often than she normally did. The two seemed to be connected in a much deeper way than I noticed before I came out of my fog. I was also amazed by Lucy's zest for life, and her desire to make positive health differences in the lives of others. She was not someone I would have assumed I would become close to, and yet, watching her dance in the crowd as 2006 shifted into 2007, I realized that was exactly what she had become. We would, with and without Lena, sit out on the porch for hours while she told me things about medicine, her painting, and her own life growing up in Mississippi before coming to Atlanta for college.

"Are you ever going to come out and dance with me at one of these shows," Lucy said bouncing over to the couch, and taking the drink I kept track of for her during these shows.

"You already know the answer to that," I said laughing.

"You can't be that bad of a dancer."

"I'm actually a pretty good dancer, thank you very much."

"Then, why don't you?"

"Many people are good at many things they do not enjoy," I said, and she started laughing. She handed her drink back to me, and I put it back on the table on the side of the couch. I was almost done with my own, and it was only about a minute before midnight.

She said, "I'm done with that if you want to roam around," and bounced over to the front of the stage where she would ring in the New

Year with a kiss from Lena. I listened as the countdown began, enjoyed the sound of the crowd counting alongside the band, and smiled as Lena and Lucy embraced at the stroke of twelve. People were doing the same all over the room, but none of the others caught my attention in the slightest. I watched the whole couple minutes where there was no music, only people laughing, kissing, crying, shouting, and hugging. There was something about the sight that I always enjoyed.

After only a few minutes, Lena said, "Happy New Year everyone, and now we're going to do a new cover for my dear friend silly. They taught me this song by playing it so many damn times that I just had to learn it." I got up almost immediately for some reason I can't explain, but before I could go anywhere, I heard opening chords that sounded a lot like the ones on the Drive-by Truckers song I kept playing on repeat. Lucy came back over to me laughing, and I couldn't help it, I laughed along with her for the first verse of the song. At the end of the first verse, Lena stuck out her tongue, at me I'm sure, and I nodded.

While I enjoyed the song I apparently made Lena learn, I was growing weary of the space. I couldn't go home without spending money on a cab because the train didn't reach this far, but I could take a walk. I told Lucy what I was going to do, and she told me to make sure I had my phone. I did. The bar was split into two spaces with a front room that was basically just a bar, and the back room where the performances took place. I left the backroom and went to the bar in the front to get a cup of water. The lady behind the counter gave me one for free, but I tipped her anyway while trying to figure out what to do. The front room was still very loud so I decided to step outside, and see if maybe there was a coffee shop or something nearby since I couldn't remember. I stepped outside and stood beside the door on the right side of the front window surveying the street and the shops around me.

There were a couple of picnic tables at the end of the block in front of a store that was only open during the day, and I decided that might be a nice place to relax. Cars passed by on the street as I walked past an antique shop, a yogurt place where you fixed your own sundae and added whatever toppings you wanted, and a closet-sized restaurant that sold pizza by the slice. I passed another bar called Flagship and found myself in front of what appeared to be a thrift store. I took a seat on the top of one of the picnic tables, lit a smoke, and once again made sure I had my phone in my pocket. People walked by me from either direction for a few minutes, and I imagined what bar or house or restaurant they were coming from or heading to. It was a fun game, and one I often played when I went out with friends and then disappeared on my own. I was convincing myself that a young African American couple had a lovely dinner when I heard a voice that I only barely recognized coming from the opposite direction of the bar I'd just left.

"You're not going to try to knock me off the sidewalk are you," she said laughing, and stopping in front of me.

Smiling more than I would have expected, I said, "No, but I would love to apologize for last time if you're willing to hear it."

"Why don't we call it even," she asked pointing at the picnic table.

I nodded, and as she sat down beside me, I asked, "Even?"

"I kind of read you the riot act for what was probably an accident."

"True," I said smiling, "But I wasn't paying attention, and I could have hurt you."

"So, call it even?"

"Sounds good to me."

"I'm Rose," she said, and I started laughing. "What," she said staring at me.

"I was just thinking about your shirt the other day, it seemed funny."

"I love those things."

"A lot of people do," I said thinking about Jordan and Abs' parents. "Everybody just calls me Kid."

"Do you like that," she asked.

"I prefer it."

"Nice to meet you Kid."

"Same to you Rose of the Palmetto Rose t-shirt."

"You're having some fun with that shirt."

"It's a long story," I said and started laughing again. "What are you up to?"

"I was out celebrating the New Year with friends, and I just wanted some time to myself so I took a walk in the park over there," she said pointing in the direction where she had come from to a grass expanse that was just barely recognizable from where we sat.

"Same here, well, the wanting some time to myself part."

"You should check out this band playing down the block, Faint Praise, they're one of my favorites in the whole city." I couldn't help it, I started laughing again. "What now," she said smacking me on the shoulder. It took me a few minutes to respond.

Finally, once the laughter died down, I said, "That's my best friend's band, I was camped on the couch listening to the show until right after midnight." Lena had come up with the name one night years ago when Greg asked her what she wanted from her music career. She said she wanted enough money to pay the rent, enough popularity to never need to sleep alone, and just a bit of faint praise. Thinking about that night, it struck me that maybe the reason I thought of those years as a "fog" was because all the memories from that time seemed somehow darker like they were shrouded or covered or muted in my mind somehow. I didn't know.

"Really? We were in the front room dancing and playing darts," she says finally getting to share my laughter, "Your friend is awesome!"

"She really is, sometimes," I say continuing to chuckle. "Except when she tries to make me blush by dedicating songs to me."

"Are you silly?"

"You heard that."

"Right as I was leaving for a walk, but I didn't wait for the song," she says smiling. I duck my head to hide what feels like a lot of blushing. As I always told Lena, the songs I enjoyed, the attention of the crowd following a dedication, not so much. "Silly? What is up with you and nicknames?"

"I don't know," I say, "I just never cared much for my own name, and nobody ever really called me by it after I was about ten anyway, so I just kind of let it go."

"I get that," she says smiling.

"You do?"

"Yeah," she says, "It makes sense to me." At that moment, we both hear someone call her name. We look up and there are a group of people – maybe five – waving to her. "I gotta go," she says, "But who knows, maybe we can see each other again without any violence."

Laughing, I say, "I think it's definitely a possibility, I mean, well, one of my best friends and I met when he smacked the shit out of me at a party in high school, so who knows?"

"I'm going to want to hear that story," she says as she gets off the picnic table and starts walking to where her friends are waiting in the front of the bar. I watch her go, wanting to see her again a lot more than I want to want that. I sit outside for another half hour or so until I hear Lena laughing. I look up, and her and Lucy are walking toward me with the usual combination of musical gear. Together, we decide to call it a night, and head back home.

CHAPTER 14

"Lisa is dating some girl who went to college in Augusta before moving out to the sticks," Abs says on the other end of the phone a couple months later. We have both been so busy with school, my six-course load and her continuing immersion into graduate life, that we've barely had a chance to chat since the winter break. She is now a master but explained that it is still better to call her doctor Abs since that is what she will be. She needs a couple more, as she calls them, doctoral courses, but then she will be on her own to do something called a dissertation. It sounds like a ton of work, but that's about all I can tell. I'm taking six classes because that will get me through the program faster – read cost less money – and while I can handle it, it means that between work and classes my schedule is very tight.

"And how do we feel about that," I ask because I can't tell from her voice.

"Surprisingly okay with it."

"Really?"

"Really," she says and chuckles, "I find myself more annoyed by the fact that I'm not dating anyone yet, like at all so far, you know, than anything else. Hell, even you're dating, and I'm just twiddling my thumbs and living in the library."

"I am not dating," I say, and this is true. I haven't been on a date in months.

"What about Rose?"

"We're not dating."

"Lena said y'all were spending all kinds of time together this spring, and that you even spent time on the phone with her while she was in Charleston for spring break."

"That's true, but we're not dating. We haven't been on one date, or even kissed, or anything – we're just hanging out."

"But you want to date her, don't you," she asks.

"Yes, but that's not the point," I say and hear the entire phone fill with laughter. I do want to date Rose, though I'm not all that

© KONINKLIJKE BRILL NV, LEIDEN, 2019 | DOI 10.1163/9789004392212_014

comfortable with this fact. And yes, we are hanging out a lot, but I have received no sense that she wants to date me that I know of or can tell. Lena says she does, but they've only seen each other twice and met once so I don't know what to make of that. "You said I was dating, and I am not, what's so funny?"

"Well, you know, the two of you are hanging out all the time…"

"All the time is a stretch Abs."

"Whatever, y'all are hanging out, you like her, Lena says she likes you, you might as well be dating even if you don't call it that, that's all I'm saying."

"I disagree."

"Of course you do," she says and starts laughing again. "But that doesn't help me."

"What about that Carina person, you seemed to like them."

"I do like them, but not like that so nope."

"What about the people you go to school with?"

"Boring," she says laughing, "Come on, gimme something I can work with."

"I don't know, I don't live there."

"I don't mean that, I can handle my love life, give me some juicy stuff from up there, if not about you and Rose, about something else."

"Did you start watching those damn teen dramas too?"

Laughing, she says, "No, that's Lena's game, I want the real dirt."

This, of course, is a longstanding pattern in our relationship. We've been sharing "dirt" about people we know for as long as I can remember, and I try to think of some good stuff. I don't know why, but it seemed like this was easier when we were younger. We were always trying new things – and new people it seemed in some cases – so there was always something pressing to talk about. As we got older, I don't know, things just kind of changed, and our conversations became more practical or about books, art, and politics. I didn't notice the shift, maybe it happened in my fog days when I was avoiding conversation with everyone, but I wondered when or even how that happened. "Have you heard about Taylor and Nick?"

"No," she squeals, "What's going on?"

"They're adopting a baby, which was a pain in the ass for all kinds of legal reasons, but they made it work. They're going to have a little one who they're calling Zane, and they're moving into this cool, kind of Spanish-looking, bungalow in a neighborhood called Winter Park. Taylor got a job running the resource center for gender and sexuality at some college there, and Nick is working for some textbook company that has offices in West Orlando."

"I'm surprised they decided to adopt, I always thought Taylor wanted to do the whole natural birth and donor thing like Clark's mom did."

"She decided she didn't want to carry a child, and they met a lot of teen mothers through her work at that health clinic, and decided they wanted to go that route." Thinking about updates in our little familial network, I added, "And speaking of Clark, did you hear that his dad is dating again?" Roger had moved to Orlando years before, but in the past year he met another man who moved to Orlando to retire, and the two of them had been seeing each other for a few months.

"That's cool, what's the guy like?"

"Taylor says he's awesome, and Clark already adores him. He was a school teacher in Iowa or Idaho or one of those I states for like thirty years and moved to Orlando after he retired. He is apparently a hell of a cook, and him and Roger throw these cool dinner parties. Roger is still living over in Metro West, and Rob, the new guy, lives over near the Disney parks."

"What about Clark, I really need to call him sometime."

"He's doing great, and him and Devin are going to travel around Europe this summer."

"They are so cute."

"No shit," I say smiling, "And Charlotte and Lori are getting married, well, you know, not legally because it's America, but they're having a ceremony and buying a house together so I consider them getting married."

"I would agree, fuck the laws, congrats to them."

"Do you two ever talk anymore?"

"Not really, we kind of drifted apart in college, and haven't talked much sense. We caught up a couple years ago when I saw her while I was in town, but that's about it."

"So, you've never met Lori?"

"No, but Clark told me I would love her."

"You would." I keep thinking about all the people we knew when we were growing up in Carolina, and then, I say, "Oh shit."

"What?"

"I think I got a good one for you."

"Then stop teasing and tell me."

Laughing, I say, "Do you remember Lenny and what's his name?"

"Of course."

"Well, they live in Augusta now."

"They what?"

"Yep, they came back, and now they both go to the church they went to, the one Jordan went to, back then."

"How do you know this, have you talked to them?"

"Nope, Lena got me on this face thing site, I don't know how it works, and Lenny was on there too so we connected, and he told me they came back because he got a good job at the nuclear plant doing something to do with engineering that I didn't understand all that well." I smile thinking about receiving the message from Lenny, and add, "They're still together, and living in one of those old-fashioned houses up on the hill near the college."

"That's the college that Sabrina girl went to."

"Are we sure we're cool with Lisa dating her?"

"Shut up," Abs says laughing, and adds, "Okay, maybe I'm a little, but just a little, jealous, okay, maybe just a little, you know, I don't know, it's hard to explain."

"You don't have to talk about it if you don't want to."

"You better say that," she says laughing, "We waited forever on you."

"True, and thanks again."

"No problem, but I don't know, you know, I love Lisa and always will, but I think, and don't you say it because I know this was stupid and not fair at all, okay, I got it, but I think I expected her to spend a little time in Milledgeville, and then get bored. I thought she'd be down here with me by now, I know, I know, but I did, you know, and now she's talking about opening a book store up there in bum-fucked-Egypt and dating this Sabrina chick and I just don't know, I don't like it, but I also don't want to move to the middle of nowhere if I can help it, and I just, I don't know okay, she was supposed to come back to me, but I don't think she's going to."

A couple decades of experience tell me Abs has her pouty look right now and may even be kicking the dirt if there is anything to kick. "I get it," I say in my softest voice.

"I guess I just always figured we were it, you know, I thought we'd do our own thing and then come back together, but now I don't think that's going to happen, and what's worse, okay maybe not worse, but it feels that way, you know," she says and I affirm that I know whatever she wants me to know, "I just, okay, what's worse is that I don't even think that I would want us back together, you know, we've both changed so much since she moved there and I moved here and started this program. I don't think we would fit anymore, you know, but at the same time, it still kind of sucks to think about us as done, you know, romantically over I guess."

"I think that actually makes a lot of sense Abs," I say smiling, "And the Sabrina girl?"

"You know what, I think it bothers me that she's pretty cool, you know, I talked to her on the phone one night, you know, gave her the overprotective parent third degree type thing, you know, because Lisa is awesome and important, and I think it bothers me that she's kind of cool, you know, I don't know, I guess I like her, but I'm not ready to like that I like her."

Laughing more than I expected, I say, "I could see how that would be a problem."

"It's just confusing."

"It could be worse," I say remembering another tidbit of gossip that I think Abs would appreciate. "I mean, you could be Becca."

"Becca, ooh, what is she doing now?"

"She's still living in rural Texas, though the baby daddy is long gone and now she has three rug rats instead of one."

"Facebook?"

"Is that what it's called?"

"I just realized something," Abs says laughing.

"What?"

"You're more fun to talk to when I can punch you for saying stupid things."

"I love you too."

"Well, speaking of social media stuff, did you reconnect with Lindsay or Jessica?"

"Nope, no clue what is going on with either one of them, hell, I only learned about Becca through pictures she was posting on the page thing, and then Lenny filled in some details because it turns out his parents are friends with her parents."

"Well, I don't know about Jessica, but Lindsay is in college like you."

"Really?"

"Yep, she's at the school that girl Sabrina went to. She reached out to me for advice on courses, and we spent like two hours on the phone catching up. She's doing great."

"I can't think about her without thinking of her brother's pretty thing, is that strange?"

"See, I really need to be able to punch you."

CHAPTER 15

The summer of 2007 went faster than seemed possible. After taking six classes in the spring, the four I took in two different summer sessions seemed almost like a vacation despite the amount of work and the shortened length of the classes. I was sitting outside near the end of the second summer session thinking about the first course reading from a literature class that I had not read before the class when Rose said, "Someone is really focused today."

"Shouldn't you be in class missy," I asked without looking up from the book.

"We got out early. What about you?"

"Ours was cancelled today, which I guess is appropriate."

"Why is it appropriate?"

"Because this is the first book I haven't read beforehand that is being covered in one of my literature classes so I was actually really excited about it." Laughing, she sits down beside me and shakes her head. "I know, I know, but it bothers me," I say smiling. I'm getting more and more comfortable spending time with Rose. After starting 2007 with a conversation on a picnic table, we've been in somewhat constant contact, at least in terms of communication. We trade notes and laugh about classes. We meet up when we're going to the same party or concert or bookstore. We talk on the phone at least a few nights a week, and we hang out on campus with each other, best I can tell, more than with anyone else.

At the same time, I'm still not sure what we are to each other. I know I like her a lot, and like Lena did from the start, I've begun to feel like I see signs that she feels the same way. Neither of us have done anything about it yet, though, and I don't know what to make of that. I know for me it comes down to the fear thing, and the fact that she's the person I've liked most since Jordan. I'm terrified of her to be honest, but I don't know what's going on with her. Sometimes I think maybe it's the same kind of thing, but since I haven't talked to her about how I feel or about Jordan in detail, I have no clue. She

© KONINKLIJKE BRILL NV, LEIDEN, 2019 | DOI 10.1163/9789004392212_015

knows that Jordan died, and I know that she had a tough childhood in Charleston, but that's about as far as we've gotten into the more difficult topics so I don't know. Other times I think maybe she just sees me as a friend, and that would be awesome too, I think, but again, I'm not sure. She's not seeing anyone else. I'm not seeing anyone else. But I'm not sure if we're seeing each other or not. I finally decided, after talking it over with both Lena and Abs, that I'm just going to ask her out soon, and see what happens. The not knowing is just kind of driving me crazy at this point.

"You are a funny one," she says as another student I know walks by where we're sitting and waves while saying hey to me. I chuckle because he calls me Kid, and yet, for the life of me, I cannot remember his name no matter how hard I try. "Hey," she says after he passes us, "What is the deal with the Kid thing, like, for real, what is that?"

"It's a nickname, you know that."

"Yes, I know that, of course, but where did it come from?"

I run my hand through my hair and shake an ash off my skirt. This is not a subject I normally talk about, or even think about. I've been "Kid" or simply avoided using a name as best I can or been Lena's "Silly" for as long as I can remember, and most people just take it in stride or show me right away they won't fit in my life if they can't handle freedom of names. Surprising myself, I open my mouth to make some excuse for why I don't like to talk about it, and instead, I say, "My first love called me Kid when we were first getting to know each other, and it kind of stuck."

"Like you're other first love calling you Silly?"

"Yeah, kind of like that."

"Why did he call you Kid," she asks and looks deep into my eyes. I'm surprised I am even talking about this, but since I've started, I figure, what the hell.

"He was a little, and I mean a little, not even a year, older than I was. He thought this was funny, and maybe even important, I'm not sure, but he would never let me forget it. He called me Kid because I was, as he put it when we were both eight though he was a few months older, "so much younger" than him that he should be careful with me. It was a joke, and it became a running joke between the two of us the first couple years we knew each other. His mom would ask where he was going, and he would tell her out with some kid from soccer. I liked that he had a special name for me, I guess, I mean, I don't know, we had to hide everything even then, and I guess it made me feel more special and made what we had seem more okay because at first only he called me that, and I just kind of liked it."

She nods, and I continue, "I don't really remember how it became my name all the time, I mean, I think it started one day out at the river near where I lived. I was meeting my friend Abs, we weren't speaking at school because everyone thought we were a couple, and she wanted them to stop thinking that. I didn't care because Lena and Jordan didn't go to school with us, and I didn't care if other girls or boys noticed me if that makes any sense." She nods again, "Well, we were sitting on the river one day, and Abs was cutting open a can of soda, she never opened them the normal way, and I got up to stretch, I mean, we had been there a while already, and when I got up, one of Jordan's notes fell out of my pocket and Abs picked it up."

"I bet you were scared," Rose says taking my hand.

"I was," I say softly, "I didn't have any reason to be, but I didn't know that yet, I mean, no one other than Lena and Jordan knew anything at that point, and so Abs is holding this letter, but I thought maybe it was okay because we never put our own names on the letters, we used code. I wrote to Play because he loved the group Kid 'N Play, and I thought it was funny to do that since he called me Kid. I mean, we were so young and goofy Rose, I mean, it sounds absurd to me now, but we had all these little codes and safeguards to make sure we didn't get caught."

"I get it," Rose says smiling at me.

"So, Abs has this letter from Play to Kid, I mean it just sounds so funny now, but at the time, it was a different feeling. Anyway, she looks at me puzzled, I mean, of course she was puzzled because I rarely talked to anyone so who was I writing notes to? I came up with the best excuse I could think of, I said I was writing to myself, like my future self. My handwriting was a lot like Jordan's at that point, so I hoped that would be it. I was shocked that it worked, and when she asked, I said that I kind of wanted to be a kid forever and thought about going by Kid since I didn't like my own name, I mean, it was the best I could come up with at the time. For some reason, maybe because she was such a free spirit herself, maybe because she always loved me even when I wasn't sure if we shared that fact in all things, I don't know, she bought it, and I remember her calling me Kid at school a few weeks later. Over time, I don't know, it just kind of became my name, I even requested it from teachers in classes – I still do – and especially after, well, after Jordan, you know, somehow the name meant even more to me."

I still remembered when Abs figured all this out years later. It was right after I told her how I felt about Jordan in a parking lot near where we lived, and she came over one night when I was sitting on the back porch. She laughed so hard when I confirmed her suspicions and admitted that she still remembered how strange it seemed that I just made up a nickname for the hell of it. She remembered deciding that if it was important to me, that was good enough. I remembered worrying for about two weeks because I thought she would see through my story. Together, teenagers on a back porch, we had a lot of good laughs about the whole thing. I was reliving that night on the back porch in my head when Rose said, "I think that makes sense, like, maybe it's like the tattoo and the letters you write now, it's a way you keep him with you."

"That's my best guess," I say smiling and enjoying the feeling of our hands touching more than I'm entirely comfortable with.

"I get it," she says smiling, "Like, well, this is not something I tell a lot of people, but I didn't always go by Rose, I started using this name after high school."

"Really," I say surprised, "Why did you pick Rose?"

"When I was a little girl, talk about goofy kid stuff right, there was this little girl playing in our front yard with these Palmetto Roses that I'm guessing her parents bought her or something, and she looked so happy, like, happier than anyone I'd ever seen before in my life." Her hazel eyes shine as she speaks, and she rubs her legs over the dark blue jeans she is wearing. She smiles as big as I would guess she can, and says, "I loved how happy she was, I just loved it, so I started collecting Palmetto Roses, and I took one of them like everywhere for years." The fact that I had learned over the past few months that she had a few of those shirts like the ones Abs and I had was starting to make a lot more sense. "I don't know, in my little head, I guess it became a symbol of happiness, like, something to aspire to, and so when I became an adult, I thought it would be cool if I was a Rose myself."

"I like that," I said watching her blush.

"And I like your name," she says, "Especially now that I know where it comes from."

"What do you mean?"

"Well," she says, "It's not just a name, it's like my name, it's something special you picked that says something important, though also not available to everyone, about who you are and where you've been in your life."

"Huh," I say shaking my head, "I guess it does." I don't know why, but this felt like the right moment. She was looking at me with a softness in her eyes. I was looking back at her, and I could feel blush already visible on my cheeks. We were holding hands. We were sharing parts of our stories that we didn't share with everyone. I distinctly remember thinking there was never going to be a more fitting time to find out what this was. I closed my eyes, took a deep breath, and before fear could stop me, I said, "Hey Rose?"

"Yeah Kid."

"Do you think, or would you like to, I mean, do you think we could maybe go out sometime, I mean, like on a date or something like that?"

CHAPTER 16

"You sure we got enough wine for the night," Greg asks walking out on the porch of mine and Lena's place three weeks later. The three of us are camped out on the porch and have been for a few hours. A Ryan Adams album, appropriately titled *Heartbreaker*, plays on repeat in Lena's CD player, and Greg is already well passed tipsy though, as usual, he says he's just a little buzzed. We are drinking various brands of pinot that I picked up from the grocery store specifically for this night. Lena is in her favorite chair tapping cigarette ashes and smiling at Greg. I'm in the third chair so Greg can sit between us tonight. Sullivan has probably already arrived in Possibilities where he will take over his childhood church, and we are helping Greg handle the goodbye as best we can.

Lena's phone goes off as Greg sits down, and she goes, "I don't need this right now," before chuckling and putting the phone back in her pocket.

"Anything good," Greg asks slurring his speech a bit.

"Just that guy Mitch from the other night, not doing that again," she says laughing and taking a sip of her wine. "Nobody grown should be allowed to be that bad in bed."

Greg is laughing as I say, "And I bet Mindy made it even worse."

"Asshole," Lena says and takes another puff off her cigarette.

"Who," Greg asks.

"The painter Lucy took home that night," I say, "Who is apparently a goddess more fitting of Lena's taste." Lena and Lucy developed this game where when one or both of them wants to play with someone else – dancing, flirting, sex, or all the above – they go together to a couple different bars in Buckhead and be each other's wing people so they can share the experience and compare notes. They turn the whole event into both a bonding exercise and a bit of a competition that I have fun hearing about later.

"Oh damn," Greg says and starts laughing. It is kind of funny because normally Greg gets a little awkward in these chats. He's about

© KONINKLIJKE BRILL NV, LEIDEN, 2019 | DOI 10.1163/9789004392212_016

as monogamous as possible and can never seem to fully wrap his head around poly folks. It is normally especially difficult for him to make sense of Lena and Lucy's tendencies to compare their various hobbies for fun. Despite my own at least more often monogamous though fluid leanings over time, I tend to enjoy those discussions the most. "You know," Greg says with another slur, "I've always wondered, do you both go pick up guys and girls and non-binary folk or how does that work?"

"Well, I pick up whoever is interesting, but Lucy is only attracted to cis and trans and other women."

"Really," Greg says, and I nod along with Lena. "Huh, shoot, I always thought she was bi like you two, why did I think that?"

"I don't know," Lena says smiling, "But nope, women only, not even non-binary people, just cis and trans and others who identify and live as women mostly or just plain full time."

"So, she's a lesbian?"

"Yep," Lena says laughing, "And has identified that way the whole time I've known her and much longer than I have known her sugar."

"Well, I'll be," Greg says shaking his head, "Why didn't I know that?"

"No clue," Lena says, "But yeah, she is all about women, hell, Kid made her consider being with a non-binary person because they are so often more feminine in attitude, perspective, and other personality stuff, and that was a first for her, but ultimately considering it was as far as she could get so far, and she has never, that she recalls, found even one man attractive in a sexual or romantic way, not even once."

"I didn't know that about me," I said laughing.

"Oh yeah, she thinks you're too adorable and loves it when you come out in the morning and say stuff like 'Well, I'm a woman today baby' to tell us how you're feeling on a given day."

"I am adorable," I say.

Laughing Greg says, "So, she sounds just like me, well, except the other way around since I can't imagine feeling attracted to anything other than men."

"You got it," Lena says patting his hand.

"So, does she have any issues with you liking men and non-binary people like Kid, or is she beyond all that crap?"

"It's no issue for her, she said she wouldn't even care if she was the only woman I wanted ever, as long as I respect who she is and what she desires, easy to do since who she is and desires is awesome as far as I'm concerned – she is the same with me, it's not a problem and hasn't been for us."

"That's fucking cool," Greg says or more accurately, shouts.

"I'm sure she really doesn't care when you end up with the Mitch's of the world," I say laughing, and Lena starts slapping her leg laughing too.

"Sometimes guys are just useless," Lena says, and I nod.

"No argument here, at least not today," Greg says, and he actually laughs a bit at the statement. After talking about it from every angle with us and with Sullivan, Greg finally realized that kids were a necessary component for his life. While Sullivan supported that realization in full, he wasn't going along for the ride. At the same time, he missed his home more than he expected, and got the opportunity to go back and be, as he put it, the kind of preacher our people need in small, isolated towns. Greg was taking it all better than expected, but it was still hard. Him and Sullivan planned to stay in touch and he was happy to have a clearer vision of what he wanted in his own life, but that only eased the heartache to an extent.

"I don't know y'all," I say chuckling, "Right now I'd be happy to develop a crush on some useless guy."

"Hey," Greg says with his best impression of mock seriousness, "I thought this was my pity party." He bums one of my smokes, takes a giant gulp of wine, and hums along with the stereo. If we had not already decided he was staying for the night, that would have done it. He is slurring his speech, has no control over the volume of his voice, and is almost falling down every few minutes when he tries to move this way or that. In the past, this kind of night has been very useful for him in the moving on process, and we're hoping it's the same this time.

"I am providing the wine, so I think I can whine too mate," I say smacking him on the shoulder. Lena starts laughing, and Greg gives me one of those hugs that only drunk people seem to be able to accomplish. It's messy and coordinated all at the same time, and a bit of drool lands somewhere on my shoulder.

"I still say she likes you silly."

"I asked her out, remember?"

"Yeah, but she didn't say she wasn't interested, did she?" Lena knows damn well what she said, but I know damn well that Lena is technically correct. She didn't say she wasn't interested in me. She said she didn't know if dating was a good idea for her right now. We sat there for thirty excruciating minutes while she explained this point. I must really like her, I remember thinking, because otherwise I would be running away so fast my feet might catch fire. Instead, I told her that I might need to take some time to myself, and since then, we'd only talked on the phone and I'd spent the whole time missing her and hating that I miss her.

"I know Lena," I finally said, "But my guess is she was just trying to let me down easy."

"Or," Lena said turning to face me, a bit comical with Greg humming to the stereo between us, "She has her own shit to work through or just doesn't want to date anyone now because she wants to focus on school or any of a million other reasons."

"Or you're just being an optimist."

"Or you're just being an asshat."

"When did you become the romantic expert?"

"When I became the one of us that figured out how to have the longest and happiest relationship any of us have had in a while, that's when." I had to admit that she did have a point there, but I didn't like it. I just wanted to get over Rose so I could go back to being, or maybe for the first time be, with my friend without feeling romantic stuff that now felt like just plain painful. It was also just kind of strange for Lena to be the one in the healthy, long-term relationship, and I wasn't the only one thinking that.

"How the hell did that happen," Greg asks as if reading my mind.

"I don't know, but it's kind of fun," she says and sticks her tongue out at both of us.

"Okay love guru," I said making my best attempt at sarcasm, "What do you think I should do?"

"Stop whining, and just keep hanging out with her. You like her, yeah, but you would want to hang out with her and know her even if she never liked you that way, right?"

"Right."

"So, just do that and if she does like you, which I bet you anything she does, then when she's ready you'll be right there, and if she isn't into you like that, which again I swear she is, then you have your friend instead of months spent only talking to her on the phone."

Laughing, Greg says, "Damn, she really has become the relationship expert here."

"I can't argue," I say laughing at Greg's elevated volume and slurring. I'm trying to remember the last time I saw him drunk, but I'm drawing a blank. He puts his head in Lena's lap, and his wine glass falls to the floor. He doesn't seem to notice, and Lena and I just laugh. I'll clean it up later after we get him to bed. I even put the kind of sheets he loves on my bed before he got here because we were sure we knew how this night would go. "Okay, but what do I do about the fact that I'm kind of scared to be around her with all these feelings, huh, what do you suggest I do about that?"

"That one I don't know," she says speaking slow, "I guess you do the best you can."

"That's what I'm trying to figure out."

"And I can understand that, I just don't want you running away or losing an awesome friendship because you're emotionally constipated."

"Emotionally constipated, really?"

"It's a fun phrase."

"It kind of is," I say. It's also accurate. I was terrified broaching the subject with Rose, but at the same time, I was relieved. I was shaken when she wasn't interested, but I was also relieved. I didn't know what to make of it all. Instead of trying to figure it out right then, I asked, "So, where is Lucy tonight?"

"She's over in Augusta believe it or not."

"What is she doing there?"

"She was invited to speak to families and patients about medical care, her experiences as someone with a chronic condition, and some of the ways patients can be more involved in their healthcare."

"That sounds kind of cool."

"Yeah, it's a series they have that is part of the medical college's efforts to shift to more patient-centered practices or something like that, and she was so excited about getting invited."

"I just thought she was out with Mindy."

"Whatever," Lena says laughing. "I can give Mitch your number."

"No thanks," I say laughing. "How long is she over there?"

"They are paying for her to stay the whole week so she can meet with families, and with some other people who study CF."

"Is she staying in the fancy hotel on the river?"

"Yes, she is, for free, and I might ride over later in the week."

"Tell Jordan's mom hello."

"You think she still works there?"

"Hell if I know," I say wondering if she does, "You going to show her where we grew up if you do go out to meet her?"

"I think so, I mean, I want to at least take her down to the river and the park, though you know they're like so different now."

"Yeah, I heard."

"I think it'd be kind of cool to show her around my old stomping grounds."

"You're really serious about her aren't you, like long-term serious?"

"She's amazing, I mean, I don't even know how to put into words the way it feels around her, how cool it is to have my sexuality and my art and my lifestyle all affirmed by this wonderful person, it's kind of like a dream sometimes." Lena's eyes are shining, and I just sit there smiling at her for a few moments. Greg grunts in her lap and squirms a bit. We both chuckle, and she mouths, "He's done."

I nod and get out of my chair. I pick Greg up, and Lena helps me direct him, he is kind of walking and kind of hanging in our arms, toward my room. We put him to bed, both kiss him on the forehead like he does whenever either of us are sick, and shut out the lights. When we get back outside, his phone is going off on the table.

"Sullivan," I say and Lena nods. "He also has like nine text messages from David."

"Sullivan's friend David?"

"Yep, that's even what it says in the phone."

Laughing, Lena asks, "It doesn't really say that does it," so I show her the phone. "Nice," she says finishing off her wine, and lighting another smoke. "I wonder what they're talking about."

"No clue, and don't ask, I'm not going to look."

"I don't want you to look silly."

"Yes, you do."

"Okay, I kind of do, but I wouldn't actually do it."

"Fair point." I think about it for a minute, "Maybe they hit it off one of the times David was visiting, and especially since David is basically living alone in the woods and in hiding, maybe Greg is being there for him, maybe that's it, sounds like Greg."

"Maybe," she says rubbing her chin. She sits there thinking, takes a puff off her cigarette, and sighs. "Yeah," she adds after a moment, "I guess that makes the most sense." She holds her empty wine glass, takes another puff, and says, "So, what are you going to do about Rose?"

"I don't know," I say and light my own cigarette.

CHAPTER 17

"Where the hell have you been," Lena snarls at me as I enter our apartment one evening in late October. I was out riding the trains and walking around for most of the day because I am supposed to go over to Rose's the next night to work on a project, and I'm more than a little nervous about it. Lena looks angrier than I've seen her in a long time, and I try to imagine what I might have done to illicit that reaction. I didn't forget to do the dishes. I didn't forget my portion of the rent. Come to think of it, I didn't forget any of the things I sometimes forget, and even if I did, she wouldn't be this mad about something like that. I try to think harder about it, but I have no luck. I draw a blank, but before I can say so, she says, "We've talked about this, you have to answer your damn phone!"

"I didn't take my phone with me."

"Why the hell not?"

"I don't know, I didn't think about it. I do that sometimes, and you know that so what the hell is your problem all the sudden?"

"You shouldn't be out and about without your phone."

"Why not?"

"Because shit could happen that's why not!"

Lena is practically screaming at me, and I'm trying to figure out what is going on. She doesn't get mad all that often and gets mad at me even less. I stare at her trying to figure it out. Why is she so concerned about my phone tonight? It's not like I always have it with me or ever do all that well at answering it anyway, what's the big deal this time? What does she mean I shouldn't go out without it? When has that ever been one of our rules? She's obviously very upset, but it doesn't make any sense to me. I stand there thinking for a few minutes while she paces around the apartment muttering and cursing. Then, a thought hits me out of nowhere, and I ask, "Is this about Clark?"

"What do you think genius?"

"Lena, I'm fine," I say, "I was just out roaming around so I could think and get ready for going over to Rose's tomorrow night."

© KONINKLIJKE BRILL NV, LEIDEN, 2019 | DOI 10.1163/9789004392212_017

I've never been to Rose's apartment, and I'm not sure I want to now. I've intentionally only seen her in class and on campus since July, but we have a project we need to finish, and she has the materials we need for the poster at her place. "What is going on with you," I ask after she stays quiet for a few minutes.

"It's not just what happened with Clark or even that damn story out of Charleston, okay, you should have answered your damn phone!" The week before Clark came to stay with us because he was shaken up after a friend of his was attacked in a bathroom. Especially considering my own experiences getting yelled at in bathrooms whenever I, as Clark puts it, blur the gender stuff, he wanted to come here to talk about it, and we welcomed the visit. We spent the weekend on the couch and the porch talking through his feelings, checking in with his friend who luckily escaped without much physical damage, and drinking some strawberry wine Lucy picked up on her latest trip to the medical college over in Augusta. "You should have answered your phone," Lena repeats in a softer voice before sitting down on the couch.

While I handled the Clark visit pretty well, I thought, I was just as shaken up as Lena – and everyone else we knew – about the news story from Charleston floating around over the past month. A transwoman in her twenties – though of course the damn transphobic papers misgendered her – was beaten within an inch of her life in the downtown area of the city. It reminded me of the coverage of Daniel's death earlier in my life – there were no arrests, there were no investigations even hinted at, and the papers seemed convinced that she had to have done something wrong. A friend Lena graduated with, who now worked for one of the newspapers here in Atlanta, informed us of the actual details of the case, which basically involved a group of hateful men attacking this woman for no reason other than bigotry. It was what I guessed had happened the moment I found out about the story in the first place.

"Hey," I said, "Are you okay?" I sat down on the couch beside her as I said the words, and she put her head in my lap.

"There was another woman attacked over on the west side of town tonight," she said, and I could feel the crack in her voice, "Or maybe it was a non-binary person, who knows, the damn news just said "a guy in a skirt" like they always do, and then you didn't answer your damn phone, and I called Greg and he hadn't from you all day, and I just," she shakes from side to side, "You've got to start answering your phone."

I immediately felt guilty about my phone habits. I didn't even want to think about how scared she must have been, and at the time, I felt my own heavy dose of fear creeping through my bones because that sure as hell sounded like it would sound if it was me. I was used to getting hassled in bathrooms and screamed at in public, but so far, I'd been lucky enough to not have anything worse than that happen when I was out and about. I knew people that had faced worse, and I'd had a couple scary moments with men in bars, but that was all so far. I hoped it would stay that way while also hoping the same for everyone else. "I'm sorry," I said, "I didn't even know about it, but you're right, I should keep better track of my phone."

"That could have been you silly," she said in what almost sounded like a child's voice.

"It wasn't."

"This time."

"I'm sorry I scared you," I whispered into her ear.

"You didn't scare me," she said regaining her normal voice for the most part, "The assholes that would kill people like you on sight scared me. You just need to do a better job with your phone since we live in a world with those fuckers."

"I will."

"You better."

She stayed there in my lap for another half hour before I felt the shift in her breathing that suggested sleep. For a while, I just ran my hand through her hair wondering what the previous hours had been like for her. Later, I slid out from underneath her, and grabbed her favorite blanket from the arm chair. I wrapped her in it, took the dishes on the coffee table – not surprisingly surrounded by her phones and computer – to the kitchen, and cleaned everything up. She was sleeping peacefully, probably exhausted from worrying, I thought, so I went out on the porch. I set down the glass of wine I poured myself while I was in the kitchen, lit a smoke, and dialed some familiar numbers on my phone.

Greg didn't answer. I didn't think he would. It was late, and he had to be at work early the next morning. I left him a message letting him know I was okay, and then I called back and left another – much longer – message promising to pay more attention to my phone. After that was done, I knew I needed to make another phone call, but I decided to put it off for a few seconds so I listened to my voicemails instead. Not surprisingly, there were more than a couple, and all three people I needed to talk to this evening were heavily represented. I looked at my phone and told myself that I needed to get used to the thing. I did this a few times, and then I dialed another set of familiar numbers and waited for the call to connect.

"You've got to start answering your phone," Abs said before even saying hello.

"Talked to Lena?"

"You scared the hell out of us!"

"I know, I'm sorry. I didn't mean to."

"I know you didn't mean to," Abs says, and I can hear a smile returning to her face. "You just need to think about these kinds of things, you know, the three of us have lost enough."

"Too much," I say softly.

"Yep," she says. "And you're a walking target for those people because with the beard and the skirt you're obviously different, it's not like Nick or Clark where no one can tell now that they've completed transition Kid, you know, you're obvious and that is scary for us. I know, I know, Nick and Clark face the same shit too, I know that, but anytime you go out as, well, in-between what the bigots will accept, it is dangerous."

"You're not going to tell me to pick a side are you?"

"No, I'm not an asshole, but you need to be careful and stay in touch."

"I know, and I am careful Abs, I just never thought about the phone thing."

"I get that," she says and chuckles softly, "And I know you love being able to disappear, I get that too, but, and I hate to say it, I really do, but please try to be as safe as possible, just do that for me, okay."

"I will, and I do," I say, "But I don't know if it matters."

"It matters to us, you know, it matters to us, and what if that had been you tonight?"

"Then, maybe I would say hello to Jordan sooner."

"That's not fucking funny!"

"I'm not trying to be funny, I'm being realistic," I say. Speaking as slowly and clearly as I can because I'm not trying to be difficult here, I say, "Look, Jordan and I were safe, we were as safe as anyone could be, you know that. It didn't matter because accidents can happen to anyone even if you manage to stay hidden from the bigots, that's just the way it is. I'll be as safe as I can, I really will, but I could get hit by a bus or catch a random bullet at any moment, I mean, that could happen no matter how safe I am from the transphobes and the biphobes and the homophobes, and I've made peace with it, I only have a certain amount of time so, of course, I'll always be safe and I'll get better at answering the phone right away, but I'm going to live the way I want to because I can't pretend that I have more control over this shit than I do, I mean, I'm not wasting any more time for any reason, and it's as simple as that."

The line is quiet for a couple minutes. I'm about to check to see if she is still there when she finally says, "Yeah, I know what you mean, okay, I get it." There is more silence on the line, and I watch the street below even though nothing is happening there. I take a sip of wine right as she continues, "Just promise me you won't go looking for any trouble, okay?"

"That I would never do Abs," I say smiling and touched by the concern I can hear in her voice, "I don't want any trouble, I really don't, but I'm just not willing to hide or pretend, or any of that kind of crap anymore for any reason."

"I can understand that," she says, "I feel the same way, you know, but I guess it's scarier when I think about you or Lena, you know?"

"Hell yeah," I say laughing, "I'd like to hide the both of you away in protective bubbles sometimes."

"You don't have one of those I can borrow, do you?"

"Nope, and the ones I get wouldn't fit me anyway."

111

CHAPTER 18

The project was Rose's idea. Hell, the class was her idea. She thought it would be a good one that we could take and enjoy together. When we registered for it much earlier in the year, this sounded like a dream come true to me. I was once again doing six classes, and it was nice to have one to look forward to over the summer. Since our conversation in July, however, being around her had become trickier. I was hesitant the third week of class when she suggested we do our project together, but the desire to be near her won the battle. As I sat there on her couch looking at a rather impressive product of three hours of work, I was glad I agreed to do it.

Since Rose was a health major and I was a sociology major, we both needed to take a social science methods class. Well, for her it was recommended, and for me it was a requirement, but we were both planning to do it anyway so that didn't matter. Best our advisors could make sense of it, it didn't even matter which one for either of our degrees because there were options for counting things different ways. We chose one focused on methods applied to policy, and decided to do our required research project on the health options for ciswomen, trans people, and non-binary people. To this end, we collected every piece of scholarship we could find on these populations in health care settings, policy debates, and legal cases. In so doing, we built a model of the options for each group, and the many barriers – though differing in amount between the groups – that each group faced to accessing quality healthcare.

We had to present this research to our class, and if we did well – though how well we weren't sure – we might get to present it somewhere else later. This meant that we had to take all the materials and the paper we wrote and translate these things onto a poster. It was one of those three-sided, white, poster board type things, and we spent the evening figuring out where everything went and placing things into just the right spot. I was lucky that Rose was good at this because I had – we learned – almost no skill at such things. It quickly became

© KONINKLIJKE BRILL NV, LEIDEN, 2019 | DOI 10.1163/9789004392212_018

obvious that my job would be to hand her what she needed when she needed it, and this system worked out well. I was much more useful when we did the research and writing parts the week before over the course of many emails, but when it came to the visual stuff, I was, in my opinion, almost useless. She was smiling at our finished poster when she said, "I can't believe you have never done one of these things before, like, how did you get through school?"

"I don't know, I just skipped that part whenever it came up, I guess."

"Science fairs, other kinds of fairs, you never did any of them?"

"Nope."

"How, or, I don't know, why?"

"I spent a lot of school in the in-school suspension program, and I barely went to high school except to take the tests I had to take to barely pass the classes. In my schools, you would get in trouble for reading ahead, but it never took me long to learn what was in our books. I wanted to read more, and in middle school, that meant in-school suspension, so I could work at my own pace, and in high school, hell, I just didn't go when I didn't need to, and went to a local diner to read books instead. I don't know, I wasn't really the "school" type back then."

"But you're an amazing student, I don't get it."

"School was boring and painful and more like a prison, I didn't want to be there."

"So, then, like, how did you pass?"

"Well," I said thinking about it and smiling at the memories, "I kind of figured out the least amount of work I needed to do to pass each class, and then I would shoot for that. When it came to science fairs and that kind of stuff, I was always able to get a C or a D without bothering to do them because I was really good at writing and taking tests." I smiled remembering working out the numbers so I would know exactly what scores I needed and exactly how many days I could miss to barely pass each and every class.

"I just don't get it," she says laughing and taking a sip of her coffee. It's some roast that is supposedly from Brazil, and I'm kind of hoping to find out where she got it. "I hated the people at school, so that part I get and it's why I went away for college, but I loved school itself, like a lot, and that paid off with my scholarship and stuff."

"I took a different path," I said laughing.

"So, would you have gotten in as a traditional student?"

"What, like back then?"

"Yeah."

"I didn't."

"You applied?"

"Yep, senior year of high school I applied to all the Atlanta schools, but none of them wanted me back then. I was planning on coming here anyway, but for some reason, I thought I might get in to one of them. I was already here, and a dropout for that matter, when I learned that none of them wanted me anyway."

"And yet, you're here now."

"Different roads," I said laughing again, "I mean, you took a year off before college, right, and I took a few years off that made college more possible for me."

"That's just wild," she says getting up and going over to the kitchen. Her apartment is a studio that kind of reminds me of one Lena had when she was younger. It is all one room, like Lena's was, but the layout is different. In this one, the kitchen is right by the door, and then there is a boundary wall thing that she has her couch against. From the living room, or the couch and the coffee table and the television on another coffee table, you can see the futon she calls the bedroom on the other side of the room. There are closets on the right wall of the apartment, and a door to the bathroom on the left. The most interesting thing for me is the collection of art on the walls – each piece is a different rendition of Palmetto Roses in varied colors, sizes, and poses. While she makes herself more coffee, I wonder just how much Abs would enjoy these artistic works. Rose comes back to the couch, bums another smoke from me, lights it and one for me, and says, "I have to say it's a lot of fun hanging out away from school again."

"I know," I say smiling and taking the cigarette she lit for me. "I'm sorry I've been so, I don't know, awkward I guess, since July. I'm working through it as best I can." It was a process, but I felt like I was doing well. I was crazy about her, but either she didn't feel the same way, or she was not interested yet. In either case, I agreed with Lena that it would be stupid to lose a great friend simply because we didn't feel the same way about each other at the same time or ever. I arrived that night planning to do my best to be a good friend, and leave the rest to work itself out if or when it needed to. It seemed like a good plan at the time.

"No need to apologize," she says taking a puff off her smoke, "I get it, and I even feel, well, similar I guess, so I understand, and I think maybe it's okay, you know?"

Chuckling, I say, "Yeah, feelings can be tricky."

She laughs and pats my leg. We each take another puff, and she takes another sip of her coffee. The song, an old jazz tune I remember hearing as a kid, on her stereo ends, and silence descends in the room. "I know what you mean," she says smiling at me.

"Yep," I say smiling, "But hey, I want you to know that you don't need to worry about any of this stuff, I mean, well, I figure that the ball is in your court now and I'm just going to be the best friend I can be whenever we hang out unless you ever say otherwise and if that is everything we ever are, I'm still lucky as hell to know you."

"So, what," she says, "I'm in charge."

"Yes mam, yes you are."

"I kind of like that," she says laughing.

"I'm glad," I say, "Because you know what, you're right, it's nice to be with you again, and so I'm done trying to figure things out and what not, I'm ready to just hang out, and if you ever want there to be anything else between us, it'll be up to you to let me know. Is that okay?"

"Yeah," she says, "I think that sounds great." She pats my leg again, and we smile at each other. "Do you want some more music," she asks.

"Sure."

"Preference."

"Anything is fine." She gets up and goes over to the stereo. She hits a couple of buttons, and another old jazz album starts playing. "I just love this stuff," she says smiling. I nod and raise my coffee cup before taking another sip. I finish my cigarette, and she does the same. She motions for me to get up, and when I do, she says, "Dance with me."

I'm almost flooded with feelings when I put my arms around her, but I'm okay too. I like being with her, whatever it is or becomes or doesn't become, and that is enough for me, that's a privilege in and of itself best I can tell. "I missed hanging out with you Rose," I say as we move to the music. We softly sway in rhythm to the tunes in her living room area. The smell and feel of her this close to me takes away most of my words and looking her in the eyes has become very difficult because of the emotions that come with it. No matter what this is, I think, I couldn't be more grateful that I found it in my little life.

"Me too," she says in soft voice, and then starts to blush.

"You're cute when you blush."

"So are you," she says as she puts her head on my chest. "So, you're not, like, upset with me about July."

"Not even a little bit, you didn't do anything wrong to be upset about."

We keep moving to the music as the song changes. Her head on my chest, and my arms around her waist, we continue to move across the small living space of her apartment. She is humming along to the song, and I pull her closer to me. The song changes again, but we barely notice. We move in circles together for the next forty-five minutes, and only stop moving when the CD runs out of songs. In the silence, we stand there still holding one another, and I hear her voice as I feel it echo against my chest, "So, you still like me like that?"

Taking a deep breath, I whisper into the top of her head, "Even more than I did then."

She pulls her head back from my chest, looks up into my eyes, and asks, "Really?"

"Definitely."

Smiling, she puts a hand behind my head, pulls me closer, and touches my lips with hers.

CHAPTER 19

"Wait," she says I don't know how many minutes later. That first kiss set off what I can only call an explosion inside me. Our bodies intertwined as we pressed to occupy the same space while migrating across the room to the edge of the futon she called her bedroom. She was breathing heavy. I was breathing heavy. My hair was pulled. Her back was squeezed. The room was silent, but it felt so loud inside my head, like an impromptu fireworks celebration started somewhere. She was shaking. I was shaking. Everything was intense. Everything was a blur. We were moving onto the bed in an easy, shared motion, and that's when she said, "Wait," and everything stopped as fast as it had begun. I pulled back. She pulled back. She sat down on the bed, but I stayed standing just in case she wanted some space.

"Are you okay," I asked smiling at her.

"Yeah, I don't know, yeah, I'm okay, I just don't think we should, you know, I don't know," she said catching her breath and pulling her body into what looked like a little ball. I watched as she caught her breath, I was doing the same, she looked nervous and maybe even scared so I thought about what I might want to hear if I were her. The best answer I could come up with was to just tell her how I felt.

"Hey," I said softly smiling at her, "It's okay, I'm kind of shocked any of this happened and I stand by what I said earlier so we don't have to do anything." It was only how I felt, but I thought maybe it would help her feel more comfortable to hear it again. "And just so you know, I'm just staying over here until you say otherwise because the way you said wait made me think you might want some space for a bit."

I realized right away that this was one of those cases where honesty was very effective. She seemed to relax, and even spread her body back out a bit, almost immediately. She was blushing when she looked up to meet my eyes. "Would you sit with me," she asked, and I moved onto the edge of the bed still leaving some space between us just in case. I asked if that was good, and she nodded before saying, "I'm sorry, I just don't know what to do."

© KONINKLIJKE BRILL NV, LEIDEN, 2019 | DOI 10.1163/9789004392212_019

"You don't have anything to be sorry for that I can see."

"It doesn't bother you that I keep going back and forth, flirting then not wanting to date, let's be friends then kissing you?"

"It isn't easy, but that's only because I like you so much, but there is also nothing wrong with it in my opinion, you're being honest, and I don't think it's up to me to decide how you feel so I can't really get annoyed by it, if that makes any sense." Lena and I had talked through these things a lot in July and August. We were sure that I wasn't the only one figuring things out, and it just made sense that, like me, Rose would make sense of things her way no matter how she saw me or our friendship or anything else. Whether or not that meant we would ever be together in other ways, that wasn't up to me the same way me figuring out my own emotional stuff wasn't up to her. "If it makes you feel any better," I said smiling, "This is scary and hard for me too, and I'm kind of surprised I haven't freaked out more."

Smiling for the first time since we stopped kissing, she says, "Jordan?"

"Yep," I say and then figure I might as well tell her, "So, the first time I felt anything for anyone after him I really freaked out on the guy, nothing bad, but embarrassing, and you're the first person since then, well, the first one where I feel, like, serious feelings, so I guess even though it might be a different situation, I kind of understand going back and forth and being unsure of what to do if that makes any sense." She smiles at me. I smile at her. She takes a deep breath. I just watch her sitting there raising and lowering her head a few times. "I'm not going to push, but if you want to talk about it, I'm ready to listen." She nods, and I add, "In any case, I like you a lot Rose, and I'm okay with doing whatever is best for both of us."

"I think that's the problem I'm having," she says softly. She is looking down at the bed or at her clothes or at something inside her head, I can't tell. Her voice is hesitant, and I want to hold her, but I stay where I am since it's not up to me if she wants to be touched or not. It is not easy to stay where I am, I notice with a bit of surprise, but no matter how much I want to touch her, it should be up to her. I just smile and say the only thing I can think of at the time.

"What do you mean," I ask softly.

"I like you a lot too," she says, and almost buries her face by looking down and bending her neck as far as it will go. From other moments, I know she is blushing in that especially adorable way she does, but I can't see it right then. I am blushing too, and I am maybe too aware of this fact. I'm also excited, even more so than I thought I would be, and that is both scary and exhilarating at the same time. "And I really like how much you like me, and the way you look at me, and the way I feel when we talk and stuff, but I don't want that to go away, and I'm scared that it will if we get closer." Her face is still hidden from my view, and she is kind of hugging herself. Her body language has closed almost entirely again.

"I don't think I know what you mean," I say slowly. "I think you're wonderful, and I can't imagine why that would change if we got closer." Honesty was working well so far so I just decided to stick with it no matter how scary. I think about it for a second as she rocks back and forth in place on the bed. "If you're saying you're not so good at relationships," I say trying to interpret what she means, "I would note that I'm no expert either." It sounds like she starts to laugh, but I'm not sure and the sound goes away before I can tell. "I guess if that's the thing, we could work on it together if you want to, or we could, like we talked about earlier, just kind of enjoy the friendship we already have and see what happens."

It's quiet for a few moments before she says, "It's not that, well, I'm not sure how I am in relationships, but that's more because I haven't had many of them really. It's more like what you were saying about freaking out with that other person after Jordan," she says, and I must admit that I felt completely lost as to what was going on. This seems funny to me in hindsight, like I should have been better able to keep up, but in the moment, I remember feeling like I had no clue what she was talking about. She took a deep breath, and said, "I feel like it would be, you know, us, it would be going for something I want that is also really scary."

Not knowing what else to say, I asked, "Did you lose someone special?" Like so many people, I missed the abstract similarity and went right for the possibility that we had experienced the exact same thing. It was a reasonable guess, but an incorrect one nonetheless.

"No," she says in that same soft voice, "I found someone special."

"Who?"

"Myself."

"I think I'm confused again," I said smiling, and this time, she did start laughing. I sat there listening to that wonderful sound for a few moments, and again, her body language seemed to start opening and relaxing right in front of me.

"You remember how I told you I didn't always go by Rose?"

"Yeah."

"I was assigned something different at birth, but I was always me. I took that year off after high school to become who I am."

"You transitioned," I said softly, and she looked up just in time to see me smiling at her.

"Not exactly," she said keeping her head up, and smiling too.

"What do you mean?"

"I am transitioning," she says and points down while starting to blush. "I'm not finished yet," she adds after giggling a little bit.

"So, are you saying you're not sure about dating until you finish the transition process?" I knew from Nick and other friends, and even from Clark despite all the resources him and Devin had access to, that our country made the process incredibly stressful and often very difficult if not damn impossible in many cases. If Rose didn't want to add a relationship to her life on top of that, I could understand that completely. "Because, I can wait if that is what you need."

"It's not that," she says laughing and to my surprise, reaching out for my hand. I put my hand in hers, and we both smile. "I guess I just worry that you'll see my body, and maybe look at me differently, and I didn't want that because I like that you see me as I am." She is blushing again, and if I knew it would be okay, I'd kiss her right away. All I wanted in those couple seconds was to wipe away any doubt or fear she had.

Even though I have had to deal with difficult reactions to my body from other people, this was something that had never crossed my mind. In a later conversation, Rose would point out that it was probably because I didn't associate much with my body anyway since I didn't feel like any of the options really fit who I was. I didn't need

122

to be seen certain ways because I wanted to be seen differently at different times – that was who or what I was. But for her, being seen as she really is, especially in this context, was a very big deal. It took me a few seconds to wrap my head around the idea on the bed that night because I had never imagined or cared what type or form of body she had in the first place. That kind of thing never mattered to me, like a lot of other bi and pan people I knew, though it does matter to some others I've known. After going over it in my head, I smiled at her and said, "That's not an issue for me, but I'm sorry it's something you have to worry about in the first place."

"I don't know why," she says, "But I'm really surprised you're not looking at me different right now."

"You're not any different to me," I say smiling, "You're the same smart, funny, beautiful woman I've been crushing on all year." She blushes, and I say, "I'm sorry if you've had to deal with transphobes looking or acting different before."

"It wasn't fun."

"Do you want to talk about it?"

"Not right now," she says smiling and squeezing my hand, "But probably at times, just like I'm sure you'll have things to talk about from the past."

"You can count on it."

We both laugh, and she says, "So, I'm sorry, it's just you are acting just like before, I don't know, I mean, did you know this the whole time?"

"Nope, it's news to me Rose." This was simple honesty again. Like Nick and Clark, there was, that I could figure out even thinking about it the moment she asked, no way I could tell at that point in our time together even if I would have ever tried to.

"It feels more like a dream or something, like, I was sure you'd at least have some kind of reaction or like a ton of questions or something like that." She runs her hand through her auburn hair, and smiles, "I guess I'm just surprised because I've seen some reactions if you know what I mean."

"I know what you mean," I said. I slowly reached out with my other arm, and when she nodded, I rubbed her cheek and then ran my hand through her hair. She smiled and blushed again, and so did I. "I only have one question," I said as she leaned her cheek into my hand.

"What's that," she asks, and I hear the hesitancy return to her voice, though this time it is mixed with what sounds like hope or maybe just happiness.

"What do you want to do, I mean, with us? I still think that should be up to you."

"I want to be with you, but we might need to go slow and have more of these conversations if that's okay."

"I think that plan sounds perfect," I say smiling at her.

"And right now," she says softly looking into my eyes, "I wonder if you might want to just lay here with me for a while."

"I'd love that," I say, "Do you want space, or could I maybe hold you or let you hold me?"

"I think it would be nice to be held tonight," she says pulling me towards her.

CHAPTER 20

"Remember," Greg says for about the twentieth time as we pass a sign welcoming us to Queens, Georgia, "People here don't know about David's other life." Greg is driving, and I am keeping him company. Greg is nervous, and I am bored by the lack of city scenery already. Greg is gripping the steering wheel harder than is necessary, and I'm hoping today goes well.

"I know Greg, try to stop worrying if you can," I say again. We're meeting David at some coffee shop in town. Lena wanted to come, and would probably be a better source of support than I am, but when David called, Lena and Lucy were already down in Tallahassee beginning their holiday visit with Abs. Greg didn't want to wait so he recruited me to come out into the woods with him. We pass a gas station at a four-way light, and begin to, best I can tell, enter the town. Though Queens is not that far from Augusta, it is a little more difficult to find since there is no interstate exit for it. As such, after leaving Atlanta on I-20, we then had to drive through some country roads to get here. Watching the woods and small towns and listening to Greg obsess over every detail is not exactly how I would have preferred to spend my day, but I love the guy, and this is a big – maybe the biggest Lena said – deal for him.

"You could have worn pants today, you know, for the locals," Greg says for the third time. This one is especially funny to me because it sounds so out of character for him. This is the main person who goes with me to pick out skirts, and I've watched him tell off more than a few people giving me hell on sidewalks because of how I dress. Hell, he's the one who gets most excited when I need help doing my makeup. He must really be nervous, I think, as we pass a tangled assortment of independent shops and chain stores on either side of the road. I'm somehow comforted to see stores – plural, like more than one at a time for stretches of highway – again after driving through the woods for a while, and I wonder, not for the first time, why people live in such places.

© KONINKLIJKE BRILL NV, LEIDEN, 2019 | DOI 10.1163/9789004392212_020

"I could have," I say chuckling, and deciding to have some fun with the conversation because I've already made that same response too many times today, "But I'm giving up enough to be here with you today already."

"I'm sorry I'm being annoying," Greg says, and I laugh. After a few moments, he asks, "What are you giving up," and sounds like himself for a moment instead of the nervous wreck I've been riding with for the past couple hours.

"I dragged myself out of Rose's bed for this drive." This was, for me, a major sacrifice as neither of us had anywhere to be or anything to do before Greg called the night before, and we had been planning just to spend the weekend wrapped up in blankets hanging out. I could still see her squirming in the covers, burying herself and grabbing my pillow, as I got out of bed this morning. I could still feel myself wishing I could just crawl back in bed with her.

"You two are doing pretty well aren't you," he says laughing for the first time today. Good, I think, I'm helping by distracting him from the nerves. I wasn't sure if I would be able to do anything useful throughout this process, but maybe this will be my role today and going forward. I can help him relax when this stuff gets overwhelming. If he gets what he wants, things will be overwhelming at times in the next few years, if not forever.

"We're doing fantastic, I mean, she's just amazing," I say and watch him smile and relax physically more than I expected. Rose and I are doing fantastic, I think, and smile at the past two months. We spend more and more time together laughing, cuddling, and just having a good time. We started sleeping together over Thanksgiving break, and neither of us freaked out about stuff from our past, though we were both ready if we would have. In fact, we've only each had one small freak out so far, and that feels impressive to me. We've spent all but three nights since Thanksgiving together, those three were times we needed to do our own things, and in some ways, I kind of felt like I was living in a dream that I wanted to just keep going as long as possible. "I think I might be falling in love with her."

"Really," Greg says stopping at a light, and turning to look at me. Smiling, he asks, "And how do you feel about that?"

"Scared at times, I mean, really scared at times, but most of the time, great."

"I think that will probably come and go," he says smiling. The light turns, and he turns onto what looks like the main downtown strip of the town. It is just a two-lane road so I'm not sure, but it does have a lot more buildings side-by-side that give it the appearance of a downtown area. "Take me for example, I want this more than anything I've ever wanted in my life, but I'm losing my damn mind about it. It makes me wonder what the hell I'm going to do when things are, you know, like really hard because this part is kind of easy once I get out of my head."

"You'll do wonderful Greg, hell, I don't know if anyone could do better than I think you will, and let's be honest, you'll always have us to help you, like with that packet on the back seat, so you won't be all by yourself in this. I know it might not help the nerves right now, but I have no worries about how you'll do."

"I hope you're right."

"What does Ty think," I ask as we pass a diner the sign calls Chuck's, and I wonder why we're not meeting there if only because I bet they have milkshakes.

"Ty is cool with it, which was a relief because I really like him, but even if we had been together for a while, like with Sullivan, I don't think I could be with him if he wasn't cool." Ty was a guy Greg started seeing in October after they got into an argument over some fashion thing that I still don't understand even though both have already tried to explain it to me. Whatever that initial source of tension in their downtown offices, it led to a date that was more like a debate, and they'd been hanging out a lot in the two months since. "I mean, it's early, you know, so I don't know, or want to know, where it's going, and he doesn't either, but for now, he says we'll just see where things go, and figure it out over time, and that sounds great to me."

"Sounds like a smart plan to me," I say smiling as Greg pulls into a parking spot. There are plenty of them, and I find this odd because that is rarely the case where we live. It reminds me of the little strip we called downtown where I grew up, which was even smaller than this one, and I giggle for a few seconds as Greg removes his seatbelt.

"You remember when Clark was figuring the medical stuff out?"

"Yeah, why?"

"I know things will be tighter for me if this all goes well," he says as he reaches into the backseat and grabs the packet of documents, "But I want you to know that my offer to help Clark out if he needed money also applies if Rose needs any help." As I did when the subject came up with Clark, I wonder what it would be like to make the big bucks like Greg does. Especially since he also came from money, he is so far beyond the rest of us in that regard. At the same time, I often forget about it because he never seems rich to me in the way he acts.

"I'll let her know, and thanks mate."

"No problem," he says, "I still say anything medical should be covered by all insurance policies and that we should have one of those universal systems, but what are you going to do." Greg sits in his seat staring through the windshield at the coffee shop in front of us. He shakes his head, and says, "Is it weird that I always kind of figured you and Lena would get back together at some point?"

"No," I say smiling even though I know he's just putting off going inside by talking about things completely unrelated to the task of the day. "I think both of us considered it at times over the years too, and I bet you're not alone in thinking that would happen."

"But you don't think it will, and neither does she from what I can tell."

"I think Abs had it right, Lena and I don't really have a static relationship," I said remembering Abs' explanation, "What we have is more fluid, we kind of just become whatever the other one needs the most at a given time. So, like her, I don't rule it out, but I honestly don't think so because I think what we want in romantic, I don't know, adult, relationships is not the same as what we want and have with each other."

"I can understand that," he says softly.

"So," I say, "You want to change the subject again, or go talk to David?"

"That obvious," he says laughing, and I nod. We get out of the car and go into the coffee shop. I go to the counter to get us both drinks while he goes over to the table where David is sitting, and the two of them start talking. The barista keeps staring at my skirt, and I wonder if she will say anything. She doesn't. After I get our coffees, I look at the pictures of what I guess are town events on the wall for a couple minutes, and then go join David and Greg.

"They don't have milkshakes," I say as I sit down, and Greg starts laughing.

"I don't understand," David says.

"Kid has this, I call it an obsession, but anyhow, Kid doesn't like to pass diners without going in because of some reason or another, and this is their way of saying we should have met at the diner." Greg and David both look at me, and I nod.

"Sorry about that," David says, "The owners of that place don't care for me so it's not a good spot for me to meet people." Greg and I both turn our attention to David, and he shakes his head, "It's a long story, but they kind of blame me for their daughter leaving this area after high school, and never coming back except for short visits."

"That sucks," I say.

"Not really," David says laughing, "I blame me too, but it's no big deal." It's obvious that he doesn't want to talk about it so we get down to business. After looking over the packet, he says, "Yeah, this is good, especially the references, so we just need you and a witness," he says pointing at me, "To sign the documents and we can add you to the list with the adoption agencies throughout the state." The packet contains, in my mind, the best application possible, especially considering the references are from Greg's best friend for over a decade (Lena), three medical professionals (Lucy, Clark, and Devin), and a respectable pastor (Sullivan). Add in Greg's wealth and clean background, and I can't imagine many better candidates for parenthood in either the state or the nation.

"What about the, uh," Greg says, "Other thing?" It is so strange to see Greg avoiding the G word, but sadly, it makes a lot of sense in the situation.

"Your best bet is to not bring it up unless you're asked, and then, if you're asked you talk about it then, I, well, look, doing this as a single guy may be difficult itself, and so, as much as I know you don't like it, that's likely your best option."

"It'll be okay," Greg says though his voice suggests anything but that.

"Well," David said, "If y'all do the signatures, I can get it in today or tomorrow, and then you just wait to see what happens."

As I sign the witness line on the papers, right under Greg's signature, Greg asks, "So, what happens next, I mean, do I do anything?"

"Not really," David says, "You kind of just wait, and the agencies might contact you or your references, or even your witness here, but they might not. The process can take a very long time, or it can go very fast, it just depends. You didn't list any preferences, so it could be fast since there are many kids without homes in the state."

"Preferences," I ask.

"Many people will put things they will or won't take," David says smiling, "Like we don't want this age, or we want a boy or we want this race only, that kind of thing."

"That sounds more like picking out a product from the grocery store than wanting a kid," I say laughing, "I mean, I don't pretend to know anything about this stuff, but that sounds messed up to me."

"I can't disagree," David says shaking his head, "But a lot of people don't see it that way. The good news for us, though, is that Greg may have better luck because he didn't do any of that stuff since he hasn't limited which kids he might want to love and take care of in any way."

"I like that part."

"Me too," Greg says wearing a big smile.

CHAPTER 21

"Let it out," Rose says as I shake in her arms, "It's okay, I got you, you're safe."

I woke up and woke her up with a scream again. I don't say again because it happens a lot. I say again because it has happened before and will likely happen again. In my sleep, I was running through the woods near where I grew up with a certainty that something dangerous was chasing me. I was much younger in the dream, but all the paths were gone or had changed. They were the same woods I knew so well, but I didn't know them at all. Something was chasing me, and after the time I spent in bed with Jackson over three years ago, the something somehow acquired his voice. I kept running as fast as I could, but I never really got anywhere. Every time I thought I was free, the woods closed in on me, and I had to start running again. This would be the entirety of the dream, until I woke up in a sweat with or without the screaming, every time it happened in the past, now, almost nine years.

She runs her hand through my hair softly humming, "I got you," she says again. I just shake and let the dream fade away like it always does after I wake up.

It is one of three recurring dreams I've been having ever since about six months after Jordan died. Although it felt like they were starting to go away, or at least visit less often, after I started letting myself feel things again in 2004, they have become more common again since Rose and I started spending nights together. Lena and Abs both thought that would happen, but I was hoping this was one of the rare occasions where they were wrong about something. I think on some level I agreed with them even then, but I wanted to believe it would just go away on its own somehow. Since she has nightmares too, often related to transphobes from her childhood and negative romantic experiences, Rose seems to understand these experiences better than I do, or maybe she's just made better progress with them than I have. We look after each other whenever one of us has, as she puts it, a "rough night in our heads."

© KONINKLIJKE BRILL NV, LEIDEN, 2019 | DOI 10.1163/9789004392212_021

I begin to breathe more naturally, more normally, I guess, and I lean into her. She holds me tighter, and I say, "Thank you," in a voice I can tell is much shakier than my usual. "Thank you," I say again in much the same way she does when our positions are reversed.

"I got you love," she says using her own nickname for me. She said it only made sense that if Lena and Jordan got nicknames, she should too. I liked it when she called me that. Abs joked that one day I might legally change my name to Silly Love Kid or some combination like that. "Have you ever thought about talking to somebody about this?" She regularly sees a counselor she says is amazing, and I'm guessing this is the kind of thing she means. Every time she's mentioned the counselor, I've wondered if this question was coming.

"My friends kept trying to get me to go to grief counseling and other types of meetings and crap for the first few years after we lost Jordan." It became almost a mantra at times, and a big fight at other times. They wanted me to get some help, and I didn't want to admit to myself that I might need help. They wanted me to talk about everything, and I wanted to pretend it never happened even though I knew that wasn't really all that smart or possible.

"Crap, so, I guess I can take that as a no."

"No," I say turning around and planting my head on her chest, "I never went to any of them. I mean, I stood outside the door at a grief thing one night, but I didn't go in." It was at a church in Little Five Points, and people were sitting in a circle talking about the spouses, parents, friends, children and others they lost. I listened to their stories, but all it did was make me angrier and so I didn't go in, I went out and got drunk instead.

"I think you should, it could help," she says rubbing my back, and like I did when others said similar things in prior years, I know she's probably right. I just hold her tight and rub my head against her chest in a, somehow comforting, circular motion.

The second recurring nightmare, as Abs calls them, is a sadistic stairwell. That's the best way I can describe it. I walk down the stairwell, it is one of the circular type things you see in old libraries, and at the bottom I find nothing but a puddle of blood. Then, I head up the stairwell, but at the top I once again only find a puddle of blood.

Each time I reach the puddle, I become so scared that I go back up or down the stairwell, and so this experience just repeats itself until I wake up. There is no way out of the stairway that I can find, but when I wake up, I usually wonder what would happen if I walked through one of the puddles of blood. Since I don't remember, or Lena says maybe I just can't access, what Jordan looked like when I found him, my friends and I decided long ago that my brain is putting the puddle of blood in my path as a representation of what I saw that night at the bottom of the stairs in that house. One of the main reasons Lena and Abs think I need counseling is because they are sure it means that part of me has never left that moment, something one of Abs' books calls Post Traumatic Stress Disorder, and that until I do, I'll keep reliving the moment in my dreams. I don't know if I buy any of that stuff, but Clark and Devin, from their work in healthcare, think it's right.

"Hey," she says after a few minutes of silence, "Did you hear me?"

"I did," I say glad to hear my usual voice returning. I can feel the shaking feeling in my body decreasing by the minute. "I heard you, I just don't know if I can do that, I mean, I don't know if I'm brave enough to just tell some stranger about my feelings and my pain, I don't know, how do you do that, I mean, aren't you scared of what you might say?"

Chuckling in a way that makes her stomach shake against me in a manner I find soothing, Rose says, "Yes, but not as much as I would if I was talking to someone I cared about, someone I wouldn't want to lose, like, there is a freedom in the fact that it's someone who I never have to see again if it doesn't help and who I can tell anything without losing anything." I look up so I can see her face. She smiles at me and leans down to peck me on my forehead. "I just think you should think about it because it might give you a place to talk that isn't me, Abs, Lena, or anyone else you have to worry about so you can just let it out."

"I thought that was what my journals were for," I say and put my head back on her chest. I use my journals the way she uses her Palmetto Roses. She draws them and collects them because they calm her and make her think of her life back in Charleston. My writing in my journals is similar – I write about my feelings, especially the depressive days or episodes, and letters to Jordan and stories about where we grew up. Writing about these things brings me a bit of comfort, but maybe she's right and I need more.

"But you won't get any back and forth in there, and I think maybe you need that."

"I just don't know what I would say, and what if I end up with an asshole?"

"You say whatever you feel like saying," she says laughing, "And you can go see the lady I go to, she's awesome."

"I guess I just worry that I'll find out I'm broken or something," I say and even I can hear the fear in my voice. She pats my back, and I take a deep breath. I don't know how or why, and a few days later Lena, Abs, and Greg will find this hilarious after all the times I shut down the conversation with them over the years, but I say, "I guess I can try it." I nuzzle her chest more, and she chuckles because I hit a spot by her left rib where she is ticklish. She retaliates by reaching for a spot on my side that sends me into fits of laughter, and we roll around on the bed for a few minutes laughing and squirming.

The third recurring dream may be the most frustrating of all because it isn't scary until the very end. Jordan and I are dancing in the woods like we often did before we were even teenagers. We are singing or humming our own music because we never did think to, or remember to, bring boom-boxes with us on those days. The scenario in the dream never took place again after we were teenagers, but somehow, in the dream we look like we're in our mid-twenties like I am now and like he never got to be. It's a beautiful dream, and sometimes Greg, Lena, Abs, Lucy, Clark, Devin, and recently, even Rose comes by and hangs out with us for a while. It's so nice that I often feel like I could stay there forever, but then, without any warning, Jordan – and anyone who happens to be visiting in the dream – starts to disappear right in front of me. I keep dancing, I can't do anything else, but he just fades away like something out of some science fiction movie, and I end up dancing all alone. This one doesn't feel the same as the others, but it hurts just as much as the other two when I wake up.

I try to remember the details of these dreams two weeks later as I walk into the office building where the counselor Rose sees has her office. I feel like they're a good place to start the conversation since I honestly do not know what to talk about. I watch the other people in the waiting room wondering why they're here. I fiddle with a slip of paper that I made some notes on while trying to become comfortable in the blue chair closest to the exit. I only stay there about fifteen minutes before leaving, but I tell myself I'm not trying to leave, I just want a smoke. After the smoke, it's very hard to go back inside, but I make myself do it. A perfectly timed cool January wind falling on me helps because it makes me want to go in the building itself at the very least. Once I'm inside, I figure I might as well see the counselor.

The inner office is simpler than I expected. There are diplomas and a couple photos on the walls, but most of the space is open and empty. The counselor is an incredibly attractive African American woman named Sheila that looks to be in her fifties, and speaks with, based on my time with Jackson, what I would guess is a Louisiana accent. She tells me this meeting is just to get to know each other and directs me to sit in one of the leather arm chairs or on the soft, brown couch in the middle of the room. She is sitting behind her desk, and I choose the sofa. She tells me she will just ask a few questions to learn a bit about me, and I answer the questions without too much trouble. It's simple stuff like where I'm from, what I do in college, and the like. She tells me I can leave my notes with her if I want, but that we won't get into anything serious in this first meeting. I like her, and I agree with Rose that she seems to make me feel more comfortable somehow. I wonder if that's a training thing or a personal thing.

After spending an hour with Sheila, I make an appointment for the next week on the way out of the office. I don't know if coming back will yield anything, but I do feel more comfortable doing so. I step outside the building, and hear, "So, you shrunk all good and proper now silly."

"What are you doing here?"

"Rose had to be in class, and we thought someone should be here for you just in case."

"Thank you, I guess," I say laughing.

"Come on," Lena says handing me one of two coffee cups she's holding, and pointing toward the train station, "Let's get out of here."

"Don't have to tell me twice."

Together, we start walking down the sidewalk, and after about a block, she says, "I'm proud of you for doing this."

"Walking with you, well, yeah, it can be embarrassing to be seen with you, but I love you anyway."

Laughing, she says, "You know what I mean."

"I do."

"So, how was it?"

"Easy," I say chuckling, "I mean, we didn't really do anything but get to know each other today, so it was kind of nice. I guess she'll start shrinking me or whatever next time."

"So, there will be a next time?"

"Yes, it took me a while…"

"And a convincing lover."

"That too," I say smiling, "But I think y'all are right, that this might be good for me, and I mean, I don't know, Rose does it and she thinks I should, so maybe I should."

"If I didn't already completely adore her, I think I would for that alone," she says smiling and turning toward the train station. I feel cold, and I can tell she does too, but I also feel a sense of warmth that has nothing to do with the weather in January. I don't know if the counseling will help with the nightmares or with my depressive episodes, but I notice that something has shifted. During the fog years, I often got mad about how much my friends cared and tried to help me, and hell, there were times where I wanted to hate them for it. As another gust of January wind hit me on that day in 2008, however, I felt the opposite. There was something comforting in how much they cared and tried to help me.

A few weeks later, when I mentioned this contradiction to Sheila, she suggested that it had to do with how I felt about myself. She said that maybe I didn't want anyone to care about me during those fog years because I did not, but now that I was starting to care about myself more, I wanted other people to do the same. I told her then what I would tell her now – I don't know if that's right. At the same time, however, I can't say it is wrong either. What I do know is that something felt different as 2008 began – maybe it was me, maybe it was Rose, maybe it was my friends or my memories or my trauma, I don't know, but it was something.

CHAPTER 22

"I feel like this could be very dangerous for me," I say with a laugh as I arrive home to find Lucy, Lena, Abs, Rose, and Clark chatting over wine in mine and Lena's living room. It is Spring Break 2008, and Abs and Clark are both in town for a show Lena's band is playing. There is something equally beautiful and strange about seeing them all together, which, I guess, is why my first reaction was an attempt at humor. They have set up a semi-circle of sorts around the coffee table, and the amount of empty wine bottles on the kitchen counter suggests they have been at this for a while. I don't think I want to know what may have been said about me.

"This is our night, if you're going to stay go outside or to your room silly," Lena says to a chorus of affirmation and laughter. I expected as much, I think, before going over and giving the lot of them hugs and kisses, stealing one of their unopened wine bottles, and going to my room to write. For the next few hours, I take the advice Sheila gave me in our latest session – as well as a suggestion Abs and Lena made before then – and try to write more of the story of my youth while giggling from time to time at the sounds coming from the other room. I spent the early evening with Greg and Ty having drinks and talking about a new bookstore Ty invested in that will soon open in his neighborhood in east Atlanta. The two of them continue to grow closer, and I'm hoping these drink nights might become a regular thing over time. Greg is still freaking out and constantly checking his messages in case the kid thing works out, but he has begun to recognize that he would likely be an amazing parent.

I'm writing a rather, to my eyes, sappy story about a wonderful weekend at my grandmother's house that I think I'll probably throw away when I hear my door open. Abs says, "Your partner is freaking amazing," and then almost falls on the bed. I climb on the bed with her, and she says, "She was telling us about that health competition she's in, that shit is so cool."

"You're such a nerd, even when you're.drunk." Rose is part of a team competing at Emory University to determine realistic solutions

© KONINKLIJKE BRILL NV, LEIDEN, 2019 | DOI 10.1163/9789004392212_022

to health problems in the country. Her team is working on protocols that could aid delivery of healthcare information and resources to LGBTQ people in rural areas and who are unable or unwilling to be out about their gender and/or sexuality in such places. They devised clinical techniques for networks and online information streams that could be useful for closing gaps in access, information, and options related to basic and specifically sexual and gendered healthcare needs. Having been the practice audience for the team's speech a few times already, I think they did amazing work.

"I'm not too drunk to punch you," she slurs.

"Where's Dre," I ask. Dre is a first-year graduate student, I think he's in Abs' program too, but he may be in another, that she has been seeing casually. She calls him her sexy friend, and swears he has the most beautiful legs ever. "I thought he was coming up with you."

"Duh, he did come up with me."

"Then, where is he?"

"He's visiting his friends stupid," she slurs before putting her head in my lap. "Kid," she says, and I look down at her, "I'm dizzy."

"I bet you are," I say laughing. "So, Dre's from here?"

"Nope," she says and then repeats the words a few times. "He went to school in Augusta where that damn Sabrina chick went, but some of his friends came here for art school so he's showing them his legs are still sexy as hell, I guess."

"I'm sure that's exactly what he's doing," I say. It is only a few minutes later that she passes out, and I wrap her in blankets and go back to trying to write. I spend the next hour playing with the story about my grandmother, and even write about six or seven other times at her house. I heard she passed away a couple years ago, but I didn't go back for the funeral. She told me, even when I was very little, that she didn't think I would be there long, and that if I ever left, I wouldn't come back. Maybe she was psychic, I think, and take another sip of wine. Right as I save the story, I hear my door slide open again, and turn to see Rose smiling at me.

"What are you up to love," she asks, and while I can tell she's drunk too, she seems like she had maybe a river or two less wine than Abs. She walks over and sits in my lap. She kisses me in a soft, slow motion.

"Just trying to write a bit, how are you?"

"I'm good, but I think I'm done."

"Well, as you can see," I say spinning my desk chair so we are facing Abs, "We have company tonight."

"Works for me," she says laughing. "I think I'm going to bed." I kiss her on the lips a couple times and pat her on the butt as she gets up and moves onto the bed. She wraps herself up in the covers and smiles at me from underneath them.

"How are the others," I ask smiling.

"They're done too," she says and chuckles.

"Okay," I say, "I'm going to go clean up, but I'll be back."

"I might be asleep."

"You will be asleep."

She laughs, and I make my way out of my bedroom closing the door behind me. I find Lena and Lucy sleeping snuggled up together on the couch, and Clark unconscious on the floor. I pick Clark up, not for the first time in our lives, and take him to Lena's room where I put him to bed. He mumbles something about Nintendo, but I don't even bother to try to figure it out. When I get back to the living room, I put Lena's favorite blanket over her and Lucy, and stand there smiling for a minute about how peaceful and happy they look together on the couch. This is only one of many times they've slept in the exact same spot. I always find it adorable, but I also always think it's strange because I can't sleep on this couch, with or without them, without waking up with tremendous aches and pains the next morning. I don't know how they do it.

Since they were kind enough to stick to wine and do pizza for dinner, it only takes me about a half hour to clean up the kitchen and the living room. I don't care, but I know that if Lena wakes up to a mess, it drives her crazy. Lucy just plain hates it. Anytime one of us is the last one awake, we take care of it so everyone can wake up happy. Once the apartment is clean again, to Lucy's standards because hers are higher than mine or Lena's, I go outside and sit in my chair with a smoke and the last of my own glass of wine. The street below is quiet, as it usually is late at night, and I soak in the soft, semi-warm air. When I get back to my room, Rose is fast asleep as I expected, and

I crawl in bed beside her after making sure Abs' covers are good on the other side of the bed. The last thing I remember that night is watching them sleep and thinking about how nice it was to have so many people I loved under one roof.

Possibly due to differing levels of alcohol in our blood, I am the first one awake in the morning. I start the coffee pot at about the same time I hear a knock on the door. Looking through the peephole, I see a cute, African American man with beautiful legs. He is holding a garment bag over his shoulder. Opening the door, I say, "Good morning mate."

"Is Abs here," he says sounding like he's not sure if he's in the right place.

"I'm guessing you're Dre," I say smiling, and when he nods, I say, "Everyone is still asleep, but come on in and make yourself at home. You want a cup of coffee?"

"That sounds good," he says, and I go back and fix both of us cups as he closes the door and hangs his bag on the back of the door.

I give him a cup, and say, "I'm headed outside for a smoke if you want to join, but in any case, the bathroom is right through there," I say pointing to it, "And there are a couple spaces and lots of floor left if you need to crash out for a bit."

Laughing, he says, "I think I'll join you for one before getting some rest on that love seat over there."

"Sounds like a plan," I say as we head outside onto the porch. "So, are you a future history doctor like Abs?"

We're sitting out on the porch puffing smoke and sipping coffee, and he says, "Nah, I'm a future sociology doctor, which Abs says is your major, right?"

"Yep, planning to finish at the end of the year."

"Cool."

We sit there in silence for the rest of the first cigarette, and the length of the second. After that, he goes inside, and grabs some space on the love seat. When I go refill my coffee, I see that he took my suggestion to grab one of the blankets in the living room closet, and he seems to be already off in dream land. As I finish making my second cup, I hear a soft voice say, "Coffee," and pull down another mug for

Lena. I make hers the way I always do, but I only make one because she always says, "Coffees," if Lucy is awake too. When I turn around Lena is moving from the couch, carefully adjusting her limbs so as not to wake Lucy, and the two of us head outside together. She is wearing one of Rose's t-shirts, a blue number with a pink palmetto tree on it, and something about the image makes me feel warm inside.

"Is that Abs' sexy friend on the love seat," she finally says halfway through her first cigarette. She takes a large gulp of coffee out of the souvenir mug I picked up in Queens as I nod, and after swallowing says, "He really does have the most beautiful legs ever."

"I thought the exact same thing."

"That was a nice wake up sight," she says in between our shared giggles, "I guess he got done with his visiting earlier than expected."

"He showed up about an hour or so ago, right after I woke up."

"Abs says him and Margo are a lot of a fun."

"I could see it, I liked him, and she seems to be doing fantastic in the program and otherwise, but who is Margo?"

"Oh, she hasn't told you about her other sexy friend yet?"

"No, but I really like the phrase sexy friend."

"Me too," Lena says lighting a second smoke, "It's cuter than the old friends plus or what not stuff we used to say."

"That's how I'll introduce you from now on," I say laughing, "This is Lena, my original sexy friend."

"I like that," she says giggling as Lucy pops her head out the door and asks if we want anything. We say no, and she disappears. "I feel for her today," Lena says, "She has to do this meeting thing at work, so she'll be gone until almost midnight."

"I'm sure her annoying ability to never have a hangover will serve her well."

Rolling her eyes, Lena says, "Don't get me started, my head feels like an ashtray, and I bet she's in the fucking shower whistling and dancing already, almost makes me want to kill her and marry her at the same time."

Laughing, I say, "Don't worry, we're all jealous of her super powers, that one especially," and Lena smacks the table laughing, "But tell me about Margo."

"Well, I'm sure Abs will give you the real dirt," Lena says, "She's probably been sitting on the information so y'all can have one of your parental discretion advised, blow-by-blow conversations on the phone or walking through the neighborhood."

"We do love those."

"But Margo is this older butch lesbian sculptor that works in the art park, did Abs take you there, over by FAMU," I nod, and she continues, "That is apparently teaching even our doctor Abs some wonderful things about bodies, and, as if she didn't already sound cool enough, Margo also knows all kinds of lesbian history about like old bars, networks, and things like that throughout North Florida so the two of them are spending all kinds of time at Margo's studio having, well, according to Abs, an incredibly fun educational experience."

"That does sound like a lot of fun," I say smiling, "And what is Margo's situation, I mean, in terms of other stuff?"

"Kind of like Dre, Margo is in kind of the perfect situation for Abs because we all know Abs' life partner is that doctoral program for the foreseeable future," I nod and smile because this is without a doubt something Abs has made clear to anyone who wants something serious with her in the past few years, "And while Dre feels the same way about his education, and isn't even sure if he wants long-term relationships in the future, Margo already has a long-term life partner that she has been with for like twenty years so she's not looking for that at all."

"What does the life partner think about Abs?"

"Abs says she's cool, but she's, I mean, well, her name is Jenny, anyway, she's out on the road all the time for her work. She does something with theatre installations and stage building type stuff, and so she likes that Margo has a friend at home because she's not around all that much, and she's never been much into the sexual stuff."

"Is she ace?"

"Abs says she doesn't know, but maybe a kind of asexual person. She has desires for sex sometimes, though only ever with Margo so maybe like the people you read about where sexual desire is only tied to love and intimacy, I mean, maybe like that, but then, other times for even years or more, she doesn't feel any desire, so yeah, like the ace couple, Mark and Diane, remember them, that come to my shows a lot, like that, and Margo has always gone elsewhere, but like what I do only with the agreement of her partner, for much of her sexual desire, and Abs has just become the newest elsewhere in their relationship."

"That makes sense," I say thinking about Mark, Diane, and some of the other ace people we've met through them over the years. "So, kind of like a lesbian partnership that is also poly in relation to sexual stuff because one partner is somewhere on the ace spectrum and the other one is not?"

"Yeah, pretty much, and so Abs fits right in, and has a lot of fun talking on the phone with Jenny too, I mean, Abs is looking forward to plans they have for the three of them to have dinner next time Jenny comes home."

"I kind of love this," I say smiling.

"You want the blow-by-blow now, don't you?"

"Yes, I do."

"I'm sure Abs will be happy to oblige."

At this point, we can hear sounds rising in the house when Lucy swings out onto the porch to hug both of us and give us goodbye kisses. She leaves for work right as Abs and Rose show up on the porch with matching FSU coffee cups Abs gave us. Rose sits in my lap, and Abs sits in Lena's lap. The middle chair becomes a coffee table as Abs says, "Rose has agreed that I get to steal you for the whole day, so I'm thinking we can go roaming around the city, you know, to catch up and all that."

"And I have passes for that gallery opening over in Little Five this evening Lena if you want to be my date," Rose says smiling, "I just want to swing by my place first."

"Oh, hell yeah," Lena says, "We'll just head out from here together."

"Sounds good to me Abs," I say at about the same time Lena speaks, "And I want to know everything about Dre and Margo, or just Margo if Dre is coming with us."

"Yes," Abs says, "I've been dying to talk to you about them, we're going to get milkshakes from Landmark and dish." She takes a sip of her coffee, lights a smoke, and says, "Dre is likely going to want to relax and maybe work on a paper he has for his emotions class, can he maybe just use the house today?"

"That sounds good," Lena says.

At about the same time, I say, "Yeah, he can use my room or the porch here for an office if he wants to."

Nodding, Lena adds, "But I'll have to show him how to use the printer if he needs it because we have it set up in my room with this network thing that has a password."

"Did anybody notice how beautiful his legs are," Rose asks, and we all start laughing.

CHAPTER 23

"I think you'll like this enough to annoy Lena," Rose says as she takes a seat at the circular, concrete table where I had been writing while waiting for her class to end. Throughout the summer, we've been meeting in between our classes because the combination of my job at the hotel and her job doing research with a professor has made it harder to connect in the evenings with the rapid pace and scheduling of summer courses. I look at what she hands me. It is a CD by someone named Jason Isbell.

"I don't get it," I say smiling.

"That's the guy from the band that sung that lonely love song you played, how did Lena put it, twenty-seven million times right before we met," she laughs, "You never looked up who wrote or sang the song, did you?"

"No, I mean, I picked up a couple other records by the band, but neither one of them had any songs with that singer, I didn't know he had a solo career too."

"This is his first solo one, it came out last year," she says laughing, "So, now, you can find a song you love and play it enough to drive Lena bonkers."

"Or maybe get her to add more of his stuff to her shows," I say smiling.

"That too," Rose says, and pulls out a green folder. A soft breeze blows through the courtyard where we are sitting, and it hits me that graduation is approaching fast. The summer of 2008 is upon us, I've been in counseling for over six months on that day in July when she gives me the CD that I will play far more times than Lena can handle in the coming months, and if all goes well, we will both be college graduates by the end of the year. Surveying our surroundings, the big stories seem to be the Obama guy running for president, and more stories about trans people getting attacked in public by hateful bigots. I remember trying to figure out if it was a sign of progress because at least the stories were starting to get some attention, or if it was a sign of danger that suggested the number of attacks were rising.

© KONINKLIJKE BRILL NV, LEIDEN, 2019 | DOI 10.1163/9789004392212_023

I remember talking about it with others who had the same question, but none of us knew any answers. Greg, Ty, and Lucy were volunteering on the Obama campaign and I knew he sounded like a much better option than the other party, but that was the extent of my knowledge on that subject. The news – and some of our classes – also kept talking about a developing financial crisis, but it was hard to see anything different from the bottom of the economic ladder.

"I'm going to try this record out tonight," I say smiling, "What's the folder for?"

"I'm starting to try to plan for life after graduation," she says pulling out a legal pad she had tucked into one of the folder's pockets. "My advisor says that if I want an MPH, I should be applying to programs this fall so I can start next fall instead of having to take a whole year off after I graduate so I scheduled that graduate school test and now I'm looking at options." Rose had been talking about graduate school since we met, and I had been trying to figure out what I might do next for even longer than that. I was still kind of amazed I went to college in the first place, and I never really imagined what I would do if I finished college.

"What do you want to do?"

"Well, some of the people I met at the competition were cool, and Emory has a good program that I like, and that one, Professor Hayes that I told you about, said they would love to work with me if I came to Emory. I think that's my first choice, but I'm also looking at other options here, in other cities, and maybe in Florida like where Abs is now."

"I'll support wherever you want to go," I say smiling, "Just let me know what I can do to help."

"Thanks," she says making notes on her legal pad. "I thought about Augusta too, but I know you wouldn't want to go there, and I don't know if I would want to do a long-distance thing when I just now found you. I know you said you'd be open to following me somewhere, but I'm guessing that doesn't include Augusta."

"Augusta would be harder," I say choosing my words carefully, "But it would not be an automatic no, and I still say you shouldn't limit your options based on me."

"Oh," she says, "I won't do that, like I told you, this is my career." We smile at each other, and she adds, "Augusta just doesn't offer anything that I can't get somewhere else that might be easier for you, so I'll probably have it as a backup plan."

"That makes sense to me," I say looking at her legal pad. "What is this about MFA programs?"

"I thought you might want to do that, and so I looked for some of them in the places where I might go."

"I don't know what an MFA is Rose," I say laughing.

"Really," she says, "Have you done no planning?"

"That's kind of my thing babe."

"Well," she says, "An MFA is a Master of Fine Arts and they have programs where the focus is on writing."

"So, what, I would just go somewhere and write?"

"Yes," she says laughing, "But with other writers, and it would give you credentials in the writing world if you wanted, you know, to get agents or maybe teach writing someday."

The idea sounds fascinating to me. I didn't know such things existed, but I guess I should have. Abs was always saying that if left to my own devices, I would just amble throughout the world without a clue, and Lena always wondered how I even manage to dress myself since I don't tend to pay too much attention to anything that isn't necessary at that moment. I wondered what it would be like to be in a program where all I had to do was write and talk to other people about writing. I had no clue. It sounded like the fun part of the literature classes I took my first couple semesters, and I wondered if that was accurate. An image of a group of writers sitting on a broad porch smoking pipes and aspiring to one day be half as talented as Toni Morrison ran through my head.

"Did you pick up any pamphlets about those, what did you call them, MFA, programs?"

"I have some at the house."

"Are any of them in Atlanta?"

"Yes, love."

"And they have them in other cities where you might go?"

"Yes, and some of them are low residency so you wouldn't have to go except at certain times of the year," she says smiling and running her finger along the line of one of my fingers.

"What does that mean?"

"Well," she says, "There is one, for example, in Tampa, Florida, but you don't have to live in Tampa and go to class like we do here. Instead, you work on your own most of the year, and then you go stay in Tampa for a few weeks or a month twice a year for intensive workshops, readings, presentations of your work, and that kind of thing. So, for programs like that one, you wouldn't have to live there, you could live anywhere, as long as you visited the area when you needed to each year until you were done with your degree."

"So," I say trying to make sense of this, "You could get into that program in Houston where the research team from the Emory competition liked you, and I could live out there with you, but I could still do a writing program in, say, Atlanta or somewhere else if it was one of those types of things where I would just come back for classes a couple times a year, is that what you mean?" We both knew there were schools – in Houston, here in Atlanta, in Tampa, and even some place we'd never heard of in New Jersey – that were interested in her work following the competition at Emory, and we both agreed that since she was the brains of the relationship and the one who had career goals, we would follow her career if we stayed together. For me, this had meant that I shouldn't try to figure out my own stuff until we knew what her stuff would look like, but instead, she had found all these options where I could do my stuff wherever she needed to go. I wasn't sure I understood the details, but I was intrigued.

Although it depended on a lot of things beyond our control, another component of all this pre-graduation planning was the fact that, given the chance, neither of us wanted to leave Atlanta. We were each people who spent our whole lives planning to get out of our home towns, and come to the city. We also both loved living here and had built nice lives – with friends and places we adored – here over the years. We didn't want to leave, but at the same time, if we needed to go away for a few years to get what we wanted, we both figured we could just come back later. As the summer continued to pass, these topics and concerns became the center of many of our conversations with each other, with our friends, and even in our respective counseling sessions and meetings with advisors and professors. I also spent a lot of time thinking about Abs, Clark and Devin – they all went away and still managed to remain a part of the little family we built as teenagers facing an uncertain, and often frightening, world. This fact made it much easier for me to consider leaving the comforts of the city.

"That's exactly what I'm saying," she says as her friend Kayla arrives at the table. The two of them always walk to their next class together. "Okay, I'm off to class," she says coming over to my side of the table, and giving me a sweet kiss, "Love you."

"Love you too, y'all have fun," I say as the two of them head across the courtyard already laughing and talking about whatever interesting thing happened in Kayla's life today. Since I'm done with classes for the day, I spend just a few more minutes sitting at the table and thinking about the future before packing up my stuff. I head toward the train station wondering what the coming year will look like. I keep finding myself surprised to realize that this is my life now, and I wonder if that feeling will ever dissipate. I wonder if one day I will get used to things going well, and then I wonder if that even matters.

CHAPTER 24

The twenty-sixth day of October, we took the red line to Buckhead. We didn't all go at once. We staggered our arrivals and kept in touch via text messages. Lena and Lucy took the trip early in the morning before I was even awake. They wanted to be at the apartment two blocks behind the Buckhead station when Greg arrived back in town. After having lunch together downtown, Rose, Clark and Devin said goodbye to me as they headed for Buckhead and I headed in the other direction to pick Abs up from the airport. Ty was driving Greg's car five days before when they went to Savannah and was still behind the driver's seat when they arrived at the apartment to find Lucy and Lena. Around three in the afternoon, as Abs came bouncing down the corridor toward me, everyone else – some thirty people Lena said – was either at the apartment or had already come and gone during the day.

"What do we know," Abs asked as we headed out of the airport and into the train station. We got lucky and boarded the train for Greg's place in Buckhead right away.

"Nothing, your friend and my partner won't say anything that might ruin the surprise."

"I love how we are adults now, but Lena is still your friend when I'm annoyed and my friend when you're annoyed," she says laughing as the train departs.

"Some things are sacred."

"Is Greg okay?"

"Yeah, Lena and Rose both say there is nothing to worry about, they just won't tell me anything else, assholes."

We all got the call Tuesday afternoon. It was what Lucy had long ago dubbed a "rallying cry" where Greg said he would need us all on Sunday at his house. He and Ty were heading to Savannah to see about some things related to the adoption processes he had been going through with a family for the past couple months. There was a chance that he would be coming home with a child, but as he was

© KONINKLIJKE BRILL NV, LEIDEN, 2019 | DOI 10.1163/9789004392212_024

told repeatedly throughout the process, there was also a chance that he would be coming home to start the process all over again because ultimately the teenager who had just gone into labor Monday night had the final say. In either case, he asked for any of us who could possibly make it to be at the house on Sunday.

There was no question on the phone exchanges between the rest of us that followed his initial calls. We would all be there. Events were cancelled, plane tickets were purchased from Tallahassee and Columbia, family members in Atlanta and as far away as New York also kept in contact, and plans were made for everyone to have a place to sleep at mine and Lena's, at Lucy's, at Ty's or at Rose's if need be on Sunday or the following days. Lena handled getting in touch with as much of Ty's family as possible because he was swamped taking care of Greg and doing what he could with the house before they left. Most of the family were in Atlanta, but Lucy and I drove out to Macon to pick up his niece who wanted to come to town Saturday night because she did not have the extra money or access to cars to leave college for the weekend.

Devin and Lena went out to Greg's place Saturday evening to clean everything, stock the fridge, and set out some temporary chairs in case it got crowded on Sunday. Rose and her friend Kayla made a grocery run at the same time and picked up everything Devin and Lena noted might be useful from their survey of the house. Clark created banners and picked up a cake in case the news was Greg's dream come true and got a friend of Lucy's that lived near Greg to agree to keep them at her house until we knew if they should make an appearance on Sunday. Abs and I were riding the train as likely the last people to not know if it was a celebration or a support meeting awaiting us at Greg's. This was because neither Lena nor Rose would answer the phone – instead they both responded with text messages that offered nothing more than updates about how everyone was doing and refused to answer my questions about what had happened. It was a microcosm of the playful sides of them I loved that was incredibly annoying to me at the time, but Abs thought it was hilarious.

As we passed the Peachtree Center, Abs said, "The not knowing is killing you, isn't it?"

"I can't believe you're enjoying this."

"They're just messing with you, they would tell you if there was anything pressing."

"Would they?"

Laughing, she says, "Look, Greg and Ty are fine, they told you that, so whatever happened in Savannah is nothing to go crazy or worry about, you know, because if there was really anything bad or serious, they wouldn't be playing with you."

"I don't think it's funny."

"Oh, come on, you would do the same thing to them."

"Yeah, but that would be funny," I say, and she laughs. We keep riding for a few more stops, and when we arrive at the Buckhead station, we get out and head toward Greg's place. By far the richest neighborhood any of our group has ever lived in, Buckhead also feels strange to me, and always did even when I was working in the coffee shop around the corner from Greg's luxurious home. In my neighborhood, there are all kinds of fashions, skin colors, and dialects, but Buckhead always looks like a training film for mostly white business suits to me. Greg likes it because he grew up in this neighborhood, but other than the record store a couple miles from the train station and Greg's place, I typically avoid the neighborhood for the most part since I stopped working there.

I finally got my answer when we entered the apartment complex. Up on the front porch in front of Greg's condo, there were a group of people toasting champagne glasses, and Greg's favorite Rolling Stones record was playing from some stereo I couldn't see. The front porch was packed with people, and in the middle of them, I saw Ty shaking hands with some people, hugging others, and smiling broader than I had seen at any time before. "Looks like our family has another member," Abs said as she started running toward the crowd. Never one to do much running, I watched as she jumped into Ty's arms and the two of them swung each other around the porch for a minute. Clark was standing on the edge of the crowd laughing at something someone I didn't know was saying, and I waved to him as I reached the porch, hugged Ty, and followed his direction to head inside. Abs had already gone in before me.

When I walked into the house, I immediately saw the beautiful banner Clark made prominently displayed above the living room. I stood there staring at the banner for almost five minutes as people moved around me on every side. I don't know what I was thinking, but I just felt, well, happy for my friend. This might end up being one of the biggest days of his life, and I just kind of stood there thinking about that. I, like Lena and Rose, had never understood why anyone would want children, even for a second, but there was something beautiful about the way Greg wanted it and talked about it. Conversations about the topic over the years went through my head, and I kept thinking about the way his eyes kind of glowed. I didn't get it and was glad not to, but I was incredibly pleased that this was happening for him. I was shaken out of my own head when Greg found me, wrapped me in a bear hug that lifted me off the floor, and kissed me on both cheeks and the lips with what looked like only the latest batch of tears rolling down his face in so many waves.

"Congrats mate," I said in a softer voice than usual because it was hard to breathe with him squeezing me so tight.

"Are you ready to meet Palmetto," he asked beaming from ear to ear.

"Palmetto?"

"Ty and I agreed not to try to force a gender on them, but to let them tell us what they want to be when they're older, and so we started looking for gender neutral names in all these books and online, and I don't know, when I saw Palmetto, I thought about you and Lena and Abs and Devin and Clark and Rose all coming from Carolina into my life, and it just felt right."

Laughing, I say, "You know what, I think it fits great mate."

"Come on," he says smiling, "Palmetto's hanging out with aunt Lena, aunt Rose, and aunt Abs now." His smile somehow got bigger every time he said aunt before one of their names. He took my hand and led me deeper into the condo, to where the nursery Ty and Rose and Lucy built was located. When we entered, the child, Palmetto I guess, was nestled in Rose's arms, and Rose was starting to hand them over to Abs who looked like she would burst if she didn't hold the baby soon. Greg just stopped, and of course that meant I did too, and started crying again right there in the doorway. I rubbed his back, and he took my hand. "They're perfect," he said, "Just perfect."

"Yes, they are," I said squeezing his hand.

After a few minutes, Greg walked me over to where Abs was holding Palmetto. Rose kissed me softly on my cheek, and Lena smiled at Greg and me. Greg rubbed Palmetto's head, and I swear the child giggled. He pointed at me, and said, "Palmetto, meet your aunt-and-uncle Kid," and I flicked my fingers in a little wave.

A few minutes later, I joined Lena after she went outside for a smoke. She was sitting with Ty and laughing. "What's going on," I said.

"Ty was explaining how everyone is going to think that Palmetto is his kid because they have the same skin tone, and the racists in our country will just think Greg's the pasty white guy hanging out with the cute black family."

"I feel like you're going to have fun with that Ty," I say laughing, and sadly, knowing that Ty is probably correct.

"Oh," he says laughing, "I am, I'm already planning to take Palmetto out with me, Greg, and Devin, and watch the confusion on people's faces when we say that Greg is the father instead of the two of us that look like the kid."

"You're terrible," Lena says laughing into a glass of wine.

"Nah," he says, "This world is terrible, I'm just having fun where I can."

At this point, Devin comes over and asks if there are other chairs for outside, "You can have my lap or take this chair," I say, and chuckling Devin slides into my lap. "That's right, baby," I say giggling, "You know it's always been us."

"Well," Devin says matching the laughter of Lena and Ty, "I am married to a man these days, but I'm pretty sure he can still smack the shit out of you if you're not careful."

"You're cute, but he's got a mean right hook so maybe I'll behave," I say pretending to move away from Devin in the small space between us.

"Oh, don't be that way honey," Devin says chuckling, "Ain't I worth the fight?"

"You probably are, but your husband would kill us both, and let's face it, we got pretty good lives," I say laughing and Devin hugs me. The four of us stay out there for the next half hour joking about all the ways Ty will have fun with Greg as he freaks out over every parenting detail to come. Lena has already claimed godmother status, though she has to explain what that means to me a few weeks later because all I could think of was the old movie. People come and go as the afternoon becomes the evening, and the noise inside and around us on the porch dies down gradually at the same time.

We're talking about the renewed plans for Devin and Clark to maybe move to the city when Clark comes up behind us, and says, "Awe, this is so cute," and pecks Devin on the cheek. "I better not have anything to worry about," he adds laughing.

"Oh shit," I say.

"He caught us," Devin adds. "Duck Kid, DUCK," he says to a chorus of laughter.

CHAPTER 25

"You're better than you think you are," Jordan says while running his fingers through my hair. I'm eleven years old, and he's adamantly eleven-and-one-half years old. We are lying together in a patch of grass in the woods near where we lived as children. I remember being nervous about some reading program that the school wanted to put me in because I kept getting perfect scores on every test about books. I didn't think it was a good idea. Jordan disagreed.

"What do you mean better," I asked.

"I mean, well, you're smarter and stronger than you let anyone else really see, and you don't seem to think you are, you should believe in yourself a little more." Jordan is doing his usual, as he calls it, "mentor the kid" thing that I put up with because I think he's cute when he acts all worldly and knowledgeable. We spent many of our childhood afternoons having similar conversations, but for me, the important part was just being together in the woods.

"Whatever," I say laughing for some reason, "Maybe I just seem better around you."

"Or maybe you just don't know what would happen if you actually tried more."

"Maybe I don't want to know."

Kissing me on the forehead, he says, "Maybe you will one day."

I kept replaying this memory in my head throughout the graduation ceremony. I watched with a smile as Rose walked across the stage, and I somehow managed to make my way across the stage even though it felt like an out of body experience. I was dazed and still kind of shocked that I was a college graduate. Rose and I both had graduate school applications out for review, and that seemed even more crazy in my head. I kept hearing Jordan's words back then, and many other times too, while wondering how in the world I got here. It was the end of 2008, it had been almost ten years since I last saw Jordan outside of my own mind, but I had a bachelor's degree that I honestly wasn't sure how I had managed to get.

© KONINKLIJKE BRILL NV, LEIDEN, 2019 | DOI 10.1163/9789004392212_025

I remember standing on the stage, well, walking across it, but anyway. I remember being on the stage and straining to see if I could see where Lena, Greg, Lucy, and Abs were seated or standing watching what felt like a miracle. I remember thinking I saw Jordan for just a second right before taking the walkway that brought me up on stage. Realistically, I knew I didn't see him, but even knowing that was a sign of progress for me from only a few years before that day, and I knew he was there because he lives inside me and always will. I remember feeling like I could hear Rose cheering, somehow, I felt like I could separate her reaction out from the rest of the crowd, but I couldn't remember where she was sitting while I was up there staring out into the massive crowd. I remember wondering what my parents would think, and two weeks later I called them for the first time since I left home. I still didn't really care about knowing them, but I wanted them to know about this.

After the ceremony, we all went out to eat at some restaurant that Rose wanted to try. I can't remember what the place was called, the whole day is kind of a blur, but a good one. Ty joined us there with Palmetto, and my whole quirky chosen family celebrated, laughed more than was probably called for, and drank more wine than we could have afforded without Greg's generous help. I was numb, I guess, and for whatever reason, I felt very tired. At the same time, I was exhilarated, and trying to figure out what the next days would hold for me. I remember spending much of the dinner not saying much. I didn't really have anything to say. I wanted to just soak up the moment, the people, the conversations, and the joy. I don't think I said more than ten words the entire time we were in the restaurant.

Instead, I watched Rose laugh, and mentally traced the tiny wrinkle at the corner of her mouth each time she did. I watched Abs tell stories and enjoyed the almost karate-like hand gestures that accompanied each story. I smiled while Greg played with Palmetto and noticed the deft movements of his fingers when he wiped their mouth. I enjoyed Lucy's impersonations of me my first day of college and laughed along with everyone else when she perfectly mimicked my speaking patterns. I saw Ty beaming at Palmetto and Greg, and something about the love in his eyes made me feel warm. I appreciated the way Lena kept checking on me and holding my hand at times as if she just knew I was deep in thought, and I felt gratitude for everything she has and continues to mean to me.

I was sitting on the porch by myself late that night. After dinner at the restaurant, I went with Rose to a graduation party her friends were having for her, and some of them, who were now finished with college. We came back to mine and Lena's place together, made love by candlelight, and fell asleep around midnight. It was two hours later when I woke up, watched her sleeping body cradling a pillow for a few minutes, and then went outside to think. We had some medical appointments for her coming up in January, and likely a few months of waiting – and freaking out – for responses to our grad school applications throughout the spring, but for the moment, everything was peaceful, easy, and, well, complete. I was thinking about what kinds of adventures her and I would have in the coming year when Lena came outside.

"Can't sleep silly," she asked with a smile, and set down her wine glass beside mine. We were both drinking from a nice bottle of Pink Moscato Rose correctly guessed we would like. It was the last of the five bottles Rose brought to the house to get us through finals. Lena was getting ready to move in with Lucy, and Rose and I would be taking over this apartment so she had been staying here throughout the month so we could, as she put it, "practice playing house."

"I slept for a little while."

"What are you thinking about?"

"How did life, especially after everything we've been through, become perfect, even if only for right now?"

Smiling and lighting a cigarette, she says, "I think that's kind of how it goes silly." She took a puff, and blew out the smoke, "You keep trying, I mean, you keep living, and sometimes it hurts so much, I mean, what was it you said during one of your depressive swings, sometimes it's like a war to just exist, and do anything." She takes another puff, blows out the smoke, and picks up her wine glass. She takes a sip, and then says, "And other times, life is beyond beautiful, I mean, it's like Abs always says, you ride the lows so you can get to the highs, I think, maybe," she says, "That, well, that's what life is, a long ride that can go in a bunch of different directions at a bunch of different times in a lot of different ways."

"When did you get so wise," I asked smiling before taking a sip of my wine and lighting another smoke for myself.

"It happened gradually so it wouldn't freak you out," she says laughing.

"Nice."

"So," she says blowing out another puff of smoke a few seconds later, "What do you think is next for you?"

"I don't know," I say, "The only things I know for sure are that I love all of you, I love Rose, and I want to keep writing, so, I don't know, I mean, I guess we'll see." I take another sip of my wine, and add, "What about you?"

"About the same," she says smiling and looking out into the street, "Just replace Rose with Lucy and writing with music."

"Makes a lot sense to me," I say and stare out into the neighborhood like she is. We sit there quietly for the next few minutes sipping our wine and smoking our cigarettes like we did when we were much younger. The night is quiet around us, and the smell of the cigarettes and wine mingling together reminds me of all the good, bad, and in-between we've seen together. I don't know what's coming next, but I somehow know the two of us will find ourselves sitting outside talking about it together in the middle of the night like we always have. I turn to look at her, and she turns to look at me at the same time. We both smile.

After a minute, our eyes still locked together, she says, "You know what we could do?"

"What's that?"

Starting to chuckle, she says, "We could show up Abs' parents by finally finding the perfect Palmetto Rose," and our combined laughter fills the silence of the night.

SUGGESTED CLASSROOM OR BOOK CLUB USE

DISCUSSION AND HOME WORK QUESTIONS

1. *Palmetto Rose* explores the ways past events may shape experiences in the present and future. What are some ways past events shaped the experiences and relationships of the characters as well as the lives of you and your loved ones?
2. Throughout the novel, the narrator reflects upon and works through traumatic events in their life. What do you think of these issues, and what might be effective ways of managing or responding to trauma as a society?
3. *Palmetto Rose* focuses on a group of twenty-somethings seeking to make sense of emerging adulthood. What are some ways you relate to or experience similar life choices, turning points, and events to the characters?
4. The characters in the novel form and maintain varied types of relationships throughout the book. Think of your own life and relationships, how do the experiences of the characters compare?
5. The novel explores some ways gender and sexualities may shape the experiences of people in society. What are some ways, positive and/or negative, gender and sexualities may shape your own life, relationships, and experiences?

CREATIVE WRITING ASSIGNMENTS

1. Pick one of the characters in the novel and move forward in time ten years. What is their life like, where do they live, and what do they do for a living? Compose a story that answers these questions.
2. Re-write the first chapter of the novel from Jackson's perspective.
3. Pick a character in the story, and write their story before, during, or after the events in the novel.
4. Beginning after the end of one of the last five chapters, write an alternative ending to the novel.

5. Pick a scene that the characters talk about in the book (i.e., some event you learn about in conversation, but do not witness with the narrator), and write that scene from the perspective of any character.

QUALITATIVE RESEARCH ACTIVITIES

1. Select any conversation or event in the book and conduct a focus group to learn how other people interpret that conversation or event.
2. Select a character and do a content analysis of that character. How do they talk? How do they see the world? What are their relationships (romantic, friendship, family, or otherwise) like? In what ways are they similar or different in relation to other characters? What information about them is missing and what information is presented in the novel? Overall, what can we learn from that character?

ABOUT THE AUTHOR

J. E. Sumerau is the author of six novels – *Cigarettes & Wine,*
Essence, Homecoming Queens, That Year, Other People's Oysters
(with Alexandra C. H. Nowakowski), and *Come Pick Me Up* – as well
as over 70 scholarly books, journal articles, and chapters concerning
the intersections of sexualities, gender, health, religion, and violence
in society. They are also an assistant professor of sociology and the
director of applied sociology at the University of Tampa, and the co-
founder of www.writewhereithurts.net. For more information, please
visit www.jsumerau.com.

Printed in the United States
By Bookmasters